To Thais Mazur
with my thanks for
your remarkable book
and best wishes always
Sincerely,
Iliana Winsen

28,000
martinis
and counting

28,000
martinis
and counting

Eleanor Wasson

A Century of Living, Learning, and Loving

2004

Advisor: Lee Merrin
Jacket and Book Design: Suzanne Wright
Copy Editing: Susan Jessen and Bhasa Markman
Coordinator: Patricia Carney
Printing: Thomson-Shore, Inc. - Dexter, Michigan

For information address:
PO Box 3834, Santa Cruz, CA 95063

Printed in the United States of America.

ISBN 0-9758814-0

First Edition

*To my family and friends
in appreciation for their
inspiration, love, and friendship
all along the way.*

28,000
martinis
and counting

Chapter One

All that is essential for the triumph of
evil is that good men do nothing.

—Edmund Burke

If a lifetime can be spent in learning, in sharing, in joy and awareness of all that is happening and one can participate to the fullest, life can become one of fulfillment and achievement. There is no way, however, that one can attain such goals without the help of others each day of our lives. This is a story of such a lifetime which could never have happened as it did without the love, the inspiration, and the help of others. I shall try to share it with you as I relate my associations and experiences with those I have known and not known.

I have lived for almost a century, having been born in 1908. One hundred people came to the city of Santa Cruz, where I now live, from all over the nation to celebrate my 90th birthday. I asked myself, "Why should I have such an honor?" My only answer is that I have listened to each of them, and we have grown together knowing we are all a part of the whole of this great Universe.

We have listened. We have laughed and cried. We have shared our thoughts and concerns. Most have taken action for the good of all life. Now we have come to a time in all of our lives when we know great changes are happening to cause an awakening the like of which the world has never seen. I am not going to dwell upon this, however, until I tell the story of my life, which actually is also the stories about those individuals and situations that have formed it.

Early experiences relative to World War I, seeing the first airplanes, having a telephone, an automobile, hearing voices and music from the first radio had a deep and lasting effect. Question after question aroused my curiosity about life itself. How does sound come from seemingly nowhere? Where did we come from and why do people kill one another as well as Earth's creatures? My curiosity never ceased until later when new horizons opened up for me, I learned about natural laws and the meaning of life through answers given by great teachers such as Jesus, Buddha, Mohammed, Yogananda, and many others, and especially one whom I shall mention later.

Being a typical American girl in the 1920s, I married the man of my dreams, with whom I lived happily for over fifty years. We had two beautiful daughters, Dianne and Joan, who were not only our children, but friends, and they remain so to this day.

George, my husband, and I had many wonderful experiences together. We learned to fly airplanes, traveled, we danced, we volunteered, and worked for all those causes in which we believed, but more than anything else we sought and found a great spiritual teacher who answered questions which formed the basis for our lives, giving us inner peace and appreciation for all life as well as our own.

We watched great changes in Los Angeles, where we lived, including the removal of electric trains by the automobile and oil companies, the beginning of our awareness of the controls by large corporations. We were part of Hollywood's early glamour days when George became a chief executive for 20th Century-Fox Film Corporation.

George always believed that the only limitations we have are those we place upon ourselves. When I was offered a department head position at the UCLA Center for Health Sciences at the age of forty-eight, he was the one who said I could do it even though I had my doubts. This position took me around the nation and across the world.

Just as George had a tremendous influence upon my life, others did, too, including Evelyn Davis, the Director of the L.A. Volunteer Bureau and one of the angels of the world, Dr. Stafford Warren, the founding Dean of the UCLA School of Medicine, Earl Warren, Governor of California, Elizabeth Hughes Gossett, daughter of Supreme Court Justice Charles Evans Hughes, Edmunde Haddad, President of the World Affairs Council in Los Angeles and later Assistant Secretary of State, Marjorie Fasman, community leader, poet, screen writer and author, and through the past fifteen years of my life, Patricia

Carney. Pat and I moved to Santa Cruz the same year, she to become Executive Director and I an Executive Board Member of the EarthSave Foundation, founded by John Robbins, author of "Diet for a New America."

When I first started this book I had planned to call it "Many Make One." At that time I was attending the Annual Writer's Conference in Santa Barbara where, in addition to hearing famous writers, we gathered in groups to critique one another's works in progress. As I read mine and members of the group asked me what I did in order to have so much energy at my age, I merely responded by saying that I had never drunk coffee or smoked cigarettes, but throughout most of my adult life I have had one or more martinis every night before dinner. With this, one of my writer friends hastened to say, "Eleanor, you should change the title of your book to "28,000 Martinis."

Hence, this is what I am presenting to you. It is a story of a lifetime (as I have said), which could never have happened as it did without the love, inspiration and help of so many in a setting of rapidly and continuing changes technologically, environmentally, philosophically and politically.

Chapter Two

Love is the beauty of the Universe
and its motivating force.

—George Wasson

In 1908, I chose to be born to Mollie and John Walsh, who were wonderfully loving parents. It was in Salt Lake City, a beautiful city below the Rocky Mountains overlooking the Great Salt Lake. We were not Mormons. I tell you this because it is usually the first question asked when one learns one is from the Mormon State of Utah. Frankly, I don't remember being too aware of differences in the beliefs of others. I knew I was feeling a bit "left out," however, when my Mormon friends went off to Mutual two afternoons a week. This was a Mormon after-school program. I might have really felt abandoned, but fortunately my best and very dearest friend, Isabelle, was Jewish. We managed all right and the Mormons more than made up for leaving us two afternoons a week. This was because on weekends the ten Mormon children who lived in a large Victorian house next door became twenty when the children of the father's "other wife" came to visit. While the practice of polygamy was outlawed at that time, there were exceptions and our neighbor was one.

Isabelle's parents, like my own, were highly responsible and caring people, but not religious in the church-going sense. Isabelle and I were as close as Siamese twins. We were inseparable. There was only one difference between us. She had beautiful brown eyes, skin like ivory, and long black hair. My hair was reddish brown with the freckles to go with it, which I abhorred. We did everything together, not without a certain amount of mischief, from kindergarten through the elementary grades, not always with an approving eye from our teachers even though they seemed to love us. With deep sorrow I said good-bye to Isabelle when she and her family moved to California, where she eventually married a Hollywood star named Reginald Denny, and years later we renewed our friendship.

Isabelle and I attended the Elementary School at the University of Utah, which was very progressive even by today's standards. In addition to designing labels for empty fruit and vegetable cans to sell in our pretend market—an innovative way to learn our mathematics, art and values—we planted our own gardens, went on bird walks, wove rugs, learned to sew and make cream sauce. We even performed in university plays for which young actors were needed. I still remember the joy which Isabelle and I felt in being selected to be two of the fairies in the university production of

"A Midsummer Night's Dream." We rehearsed with the college students after school and sometimes in the evenings, a special treat not having to go to bed as early as usual. The play came off well and still remains a happy memory as I think of running onto the stage in a pink diaphanous knee length tunic and bare feet, wearing a wreath of flowers around my head kneeling before Tytania, saying, "and I, and I, and I"—my total lines, but enormous for an eight-year old's first production.

Another special memory was the day we bought our first automobile. My mother dressed in her most elegant street attire to meet my father downtown at one of the two automobile agencies. She looked beautiful, as she always did. That day she was wearing a long black and white checked taffeta dress, a small hat with a bunch of cherries at the side, high topped shoes, and gloves, of course. As I was getting ready, putting on my socks and Mary Janes (the name for children's shoes in those days) my mother said, "Hurry, dear, or we will miss the next streetcar." Before long we were on the trolley headed for the big event.

When we met my father he was already talking with the salesman. He said, "Mollie, dear, I have decided to take that one and have asked the dealer to teach you to drive." My mother looked horrified, but was not one to argue with my father, as this was a time when a good wife did not do such a thing.

The automobile my father selected was an Overland touring car. Most of the cars those days were open, with one exception. Believe it or not, these were little electric cars driven by the elderly who weren't going very far. How sad that the large oil companies abandoned such a motivating power in favor of their product! We seem to be slow learners, but my mother was not.

After the four of us seated ourselves in our shiny new car, the dealer said, "Now I am going to drive around the park a few times, then I believe you can be on your own." Once again my mother's look of horror changed nothing. She sat next to the driver and watched every move. "Now I shall return to the office. I am sure you will do well even though you are the first woman I have ever taught to drive." As the dealer stepped out of the car, he tipped his hat and said, "Thank you, Mr. Walsh."

As my mother slowly moved into the driver's seat, my father said, "Now, Mollie, dear, let us drive to Lagoon." Lagoon is about twenty-five miles from downtown Salt Lake City, a recreation center that still exists today. My father managed the concessions for a railroad for which he later became vice-president, so visiting Lagoon was part of his business.

Perhaps it was fortunate that twenty-five miles an hour was about the limit, but to my mother it might as well have been ninety. At that time the road was only one way and made of concrete blocks, the embryo for the four-lane freeway that exists in its place today. If a car were to approach from the opposite direction, one of them would have to move into the open field. Most of the traffic, however, consisted of cows and sheep.

For the whole twenty-five miles silence reigned, but we did make it. As my mother stepped out of the car, I exclaimed "Mother! Your dress is wet from your neck down!" Yes, this was perspiration from her tension. In tears, she turned to my father and said. "John, we will have to stay here, I can never drive again." My father gave her a big hug and said, "Mollie, you can do anything." Sure enough, she drove home to the acclaim of her husband and young daughter, never to be fearful of driving again.

Prior to the advent of radio or television, news of any major event came from newspaper boys running through the streets shouting "Extra-Extra!" My first memory of such an event was a sad one. Our country had declared war against Germany! An otherwise happy and contented life became full of sadness, touching children as well as adults. The concept of killing people was more than I could fathom despite the parades and bands and flag waving. We learned the word German was bad and didn't know why. Celebrating was prevalent when legendary people such as the reigning picture stars, Mary Pickford and Douglas Fairbanks, came to town to sell war bonds. I asked myself why it was necessary to raise money to buy guns to kill people. I still ask the same question. If we want peace, why are we continuing to build arms of destruction, enough to destroy all life on this planet? How can we continue to spend billions on arms by wanting to wage war against Saddem Hussein because he, too, was building weapons of war? Perhaps we should look again to the words of General Douglas Mac Arthur, "I know war as few other men now living know it, and nothing to me is more revolting. I have long advocated its complete abolition, as its very destructiveness of both friends and foe has rendered it useless as a method of settling international disputes."

Despite my questions then and now, the war with Germany was in full swing. It became the responsibility of all good American women to make warm socks, scarves and mittens for "our boys."

My mother made dozens, but my contribution was one sock. The war was over before its mate was finished. Little did we know what was really happening to the soldiers who were living and dying in lice and rat infested trenches. I frankly doubt that all the time and yarn invested in those woollies did more than give the knitters a sense of contributing to the war effort. Perhaps the energies of love and concern sent out with each stitch did indeed go into the Universe. I do not believe any positive thought or action is ever lost or in vain.

Finally, on November 11, 1918, the "War to End All Wars" was over. What a glorious day this was! I was only ten years old, but I remember it so well, for people of all ages danced and sang in the streets throughout the day and night. We truly believed there would be no more war. We knew little however, about the fact that the world was not ready to make a lasting peace. President Wilson's plan for a League of Nations was drastically defeated. He knew that real peace between nations or individuals could never be achieved when human needs were diminished and the power of another nation or another individual took over. As it happened, the very nature of the Peace Treaty left the German people in a state of total social and economic disaster, the perfect breeding ground for the Hitler who emerged. Even today, especially throughout Eastern Europe, we are seeing the remnants of fears and hatreds emerging from the deep places in the human soul. Now once again our country is engaged in a war against "terrorism." Have we so soon forgotten those words of Martin Luther King, who said, "Terrorism only begets terrorism?" Can we not see that the elimination of terrorism can only be taught with understanding; just as Albert Einstein said, "Peace cannot be kept by force, it can only be achieved by understanding."

Chapter Three

The accumulation of knowledge, the discoveries of science, the products of technology, our ideals, our art, our social structures, all achievements of mankind have value only to the extent that they preserve and improve the quality of life for all.

—*Charles Lindbergh*

A few months after the end of the First World War, a fleet of flying aces from the war years came to our town. This was the first time any of us had ever seen a real flying machine. What a thrill it was for all of us as we stood together in the streets of our neighborhoods watching the acrobatics of those war heroes, those daredevils! Little could I have dreamed that I would be learning to fly such a machine in less than twenty-five years, doing the same loops and spins that I had witnessed that day.

The next major event in the world of technology that came into our lives was the radio. Today it would be difficult to imagine the awe with which the transference of sound from a faraway place could enter the homes of each of us. There were little round pads of crystals and needles, around which we would all hover to hear the voices and the music coming from afar in some miraculous way. It was not long after that my family purchased the first radio set west of the Mississippi River. Of course, friends from throughout the city came to listen and to admire. This was an R.C.A. set in a mahogany cabinet, the first to be produced in the year 1922, many years after the first scientist began explorations into the capturing of sound waves. The first vacuum tubes, later to become a part of all radio sets, were developed in 1908, the year of my birth.

I have not told you that I had an older brother. He was so much older than I that it seemed as if we were strangers. I believe the fact that my parents were totally devoted to me, their younger child and a girl, did not help my brother's self image. Perhaps the fact that my father was left an orphan at the age of eleven and earned his way throughout his life from that time gave him the feeling that all boys should and could be achievers. My brother married young, much to the distress of my parents, and in a sense moved out of our lives. While he died many years ago, his legacy to me is his daughter, Betty, who is my very close friend. Betty lives happily with her husband, Charles, in El Cajon, California.

I want to tell you about my father, for I doubt it would be possible today for an eleven-year old boy to grow up successfully on his own as my father did. He was left an orphan, was self taught, and read every newspaper, for he knew he must always be aware of what was happening in the world. He approached all life with a positive point of view, knowing all things were possible. When he was in his teens, he and Mr. Wrigley, the gum baron, were friends and were living in Chicago. During a world's fair in the late 1800s, Mr. Wrigley had a gum cart and my father had a basket. There were no concessions in those days, and my father realized that anyone wanting to eat had to go out of the fairgrounds to find a restaurant. Buying sandwiches at twenty-five cents, and selling them for fifty cents was an easy way to make money. He used the same principle later to employ young men to board trains whenever the trains stopped across the nation to refuel. These young men also carried baskets with sandwiches and fruit to take to the second-class passengers who did not have the luxury of those elegant first-class dining cars. This concept initiated the beginnings of what were called newsstands at railroad stations, the forerunners of the many shops we find in stations and airports today. My father never lost his interest in food distribution or in railroads. He later became president of his own company called the Walsh News Company in Utah, Idaho, Nevada, and California and, as I have mentioned before, the vice president of a railroad. My father was a master of energy and integrity, a loving and respectful father who never, ever raised his voice to me.

About the time I finished grammar school, which then terminated at the eighth-grade level, something very wonderful happened in our lives. It was the year 1920. We had always lived in the city, but one Sunday morning after my father had read the paper, he turned to mother and me and said, "There is an ad in the paper for a country house just below the Wasatch mountains on six acres of land with a mountain stream running through. Would you like to drive out to see it?" Of course, we responded enthusiastically.

As we entered the driveway of the country house, we were enthralled by the tulips lining the driveway, lilies of the valley nestled in cool places in the garden, and pine trees—under which, we were told, hundreds of quail lived throughout the winter months. Thousands of buttercups grew on the banks of the mountain stream, and there was a large meadow behind the house. The house had a view of Mt. Olympus with its peaks covered with the last winter snows. Our enchantment produced a check from my father and many magical years commenced. Living 'midst such beauty and close to nature became a very important part of my life. In addition to this, my mother's love of animals and flowers, her gentleness and kindness set wonderful examples. I loved my mother very deeply. With her gentleness, she was strong. She never broke a promise even if it meant a punishment.

Those years between 1920 and 1929 were mad and happy years with parties, making love, dancing, playing tennis, swimming, and riding. Just enjoying life was the norm for those "Blessed" with the comforts which money could provide. Actually, these were good years for many in the U.S. at that time, with the market going ever higher, as well as employment.

In 1926 I graduated from Rowland Hall, an Episcopalian girls' preparatory school, with my eight classmates, all of us in our white caps and gowns carrying huge bouquets of red roses. This school is now coeducational. In fact, two of my grandsons graduated from the same school—now called Rowland Hall-St. Mark's School—and one of my great grandsons now attends. On his first day of school he learned to play chess. Conflict Resolution is taught to preschoolers. If only all children were taught to think instead of just memorize, more people would be questioning the actions of our politicians today.

During that summer a young man named George Frederick Wasson, Jr. came into my life. He was handsome, with dark hair and eyes with a warmth which immediately touched my heart. He was four years older than I, with a sophistication and intelligence unlike those of my other young friends. When he spoke, everyone listened, for he had a great capacity to tell a good story with an amazing sense of humor. One day he rather casually invited me to go dancing with him. It wasn't until several dates later that he had the courage to kiss me, unlike the other boys whom I had dated. He never lacked courage after that, nor did I. Kissing was about the limit in those days. There were no "pills" and if one had become pregnant, this meant total ostracism. In fact, the only girl I knew who became pregnant killed herself. Fears kept us "pure." By summer's end George and I were desperately in love, but three years passed before our marriage. George returned to Stanford, where he was pursuing his law degree, and I went off to Washington, D.C. to attend the National Park Seminary. This was a girl's "finishing school," as they were called. I daresay they were designed to educate young women to be "proper" in every sense. Despite this title and the demands made upon us, such as wearing a hat and gloves and no makeup when we went to the city, I found my experience there quite remarkable. The school was in the midst of many acres of beautiful woods and streams. The buildings were elegant and classes small enough for good learning experiences. Once a week we spent visiting and learning about our national capitol and all of its offices. We visited the Supreme Court, the capitol, the congressional and senatorial offices and all of the other official offices. I even attended a reception at the White House. Our congressman was a family friend who generously escorted me. I have always treasured these experiences.

During the days George and I were separated we wrote to one another every day. Two huge boxes of letters still remain in my basement. I have attempted to throw them away, but there seems to be something sacred about those letters, so full of love for one another. This love will always exist even though our lives often took separate paths throughout our learning experiences.

Finally, on June 29, 1929, George and I were married in St. Mark's Cathedral in Salt Lake City. The wedding was followed by a garden reception. I can still visualize myself in a gown from Paris, and my six beautiful bridesmaids carrying roses as we walked down the aisle of that church before several hundred friends. This magnificent occasion was made possible by my mother's great taste and sense of beauty and my father's money. The whole event was topped, however, by the joy which was George's and mine as we were pronounced man and wife. Never a day in our 53 years of marriage did we fail to say "I love you."

Chapter Four

Now as never before, the world needs our
wisdom, our cooperation and our understanding
that all humanity is connected.

—John Robbins

After a wedding trip to the Highlands Inn in Carmel, California, we went to Los Angeles, where we rented a one-room apartment off Western Avenue. At that time Western Avenue was lined with orange groves, and the scent of blossoms permeated the air. What a contrast to the shabby shop-lined street of today!

A year before our wedding, George graduated from Stanford University with his law degree. He went to work for the Pickwick Stage Company (now Greyhound Bus Lines) and was the highest paid Stanford School of Law graduate at the time with a salary of $150 per month. When we were married, his employer magnanimously gave George a raise of $15 per month. We sometimes said that if we had a little more we could buy a boat and live in comparative luxury. If we had any physical restraints, however, we were bothered not at all for we were in total heaven.

To give you an idea of the value of a few cents at that time, we had a favorite restaurant on Melrose Avenue to which we would go occasionally. It was considered one of the best steak houses at that time. For 85 cents we were served a full course dinner of soup, salad, top sirloin steak (I shudder now to think of having eaten so much meat in my life) and a dessert. When we were feeling less "flushed" we ordered the 65 cent dinner, a bit smaller.

The first time my mother came to visit us she was concerned because we always had to ride the big red trolley cars which networked the whole city and its environs. This was a marvelous transportation system until the oil companies, as I have said, bought the company and demolished the whole system, red trolley cars and tracks, a cunning way to cripple a city, making it necessary to have a gasoline-driven vehicle in order to go anywhere in the vast, sprawling city of Los Angeles. I learned later that the same thing happened in one hundred cities in forty-five states throughout our country. As long as these red trolley cars were operating—this was in 1930—getting around the city or going to the beaches was no problem at all. Nevertheless, my mother returned home sharing her feelings with my father. One day soon thereafter George and I received a gift from both our fathers, a little yellow Ford convertible Cabriolet, a classic today, but at the time sold for $800. You may wonder at my spending time mentioning prices, but I merely wish to point out the tremendous changes which have taken place in the monetary world, resulting in the situation in which we find ourselves today, pushing the haves and the have-nots further and further apart. The story of the red trolley cars, I feel, is but one example of how the people of this magnificent land have been deprived because of the power of a few.

While the Great Depression hit in the fall of 1929, George and I were never touched by it. We had one another and the joys of being in love. It was also during prohibition years in the U.S. It was then when I had my first martini. An old friend of George's father, who at that time owned the Hollywood Baseball Team, invited George and me for a weekend at Agua Caliente. This was a beautiful resort across the border in Mexico designed for the wealthy and the fun-loving, who flew down from Los Angeles to watch the horse races, swim, play tennis, golf and enjoy sipping well mixed drinks from what seemed like a mile-long mahogany bar. It took a long time for me to learn how to make a martini, but since that day they have filled many relaxing moments before dinners throughout my lifetime. While I realize it is a vice, it is the only one I have ever had, no coffee or cigarettes. The next time I live perhaps I will even give up the martinis.

George and I always knew we wanted children when the time came that we could afford to take care of them properly. We had even named our first-born, whom we knew would be a girl. Her name would be Dianne after the lead in a play and later a film we had seen called "Seventh Heaven." Since we lived in a one-room apartment with a pull-down bed, it was definitely not the time to have children, so we carefully followed the advice of George's brother-in-law, a surgeon, who had said, "cold water douches are as good as anything." I am sure he was saying that "nothing works." Being young, ignorant and naive, we took him literally and guess who came up pregnant! We did everything we had ever heard of to abort. We took long horseback rides every night after George returned from the office, while I took castor oil each day. I continued to be pregnant. No one can ever know that feeling of being trapped, yes trapped, into bringing another life into the world when one is not prepared. I cannot help thinking of the men who are too often the ones to make our laws without the least concept of what pregnancy means to a woman who is not prepared for one of the biggest events in life. So now what was I to do? George called our family doctor, a man whom my father had helped when he was going to Harvard Medical School. He was of no help whatever, saying that people have children every day. His own, of course, were born under the best of circumstances. Finally in desperation, I reluctantly spoke to several of my young women friends. Much to my amazement, my situation was not new for they, too, had been in the same situation and quickly gave me telephone numbers. Since that time I have learned that abortions are not uncommon. Frightened, but determined, I called one of the telephone numbers and the next day George and I drove to an office in downtown Los Angeles. We took an elevator to the designated floor and entered a tiny office where we found one man and no nurse. He immediately asked for a hundred dollars in cash, and ushered me into a small room that contained only a brown leather couch. He proceeded in a cool manner with no anesthetic. I well remember when I cried out in pain, he reproached me by saying, "Keep quiet, you will be heard in the next office!" The botchy job he performed resulted in major surgery several years later. We drove home quietly, with feelings of sadness and relief. I feel my own experience was merely but one of millions which were comparable and would happen again if Roe vs. Wade is reversed.

Since George was at the office every weekday, I decided to return to college. I signed up as a student at UCLA, to become a member of the class of 1930. I also began exploring volunteer opportunities. At that time, however, I found it very difficult to have the gifts of time and concern acceptable in public institutions. At that time there were no directors of volunteer bureaus to help match the persons with the needs. A friend and I visited all the orphanages in Los Angeles to offer our services, with no acceptance. Little did they appreciate that if we had been given an opportunity to do the menial things, more of their time could have been given to the children. Finally a friend suggested I go to the Assistance League in Hollywood. This I did and found a warm welcome. They needed to have someone visit various homes to learn whether or not those making requests for food really needed it. Remember this was during the depression years and people were going hungry, and many stood on street corners selling apples in order to make a few cents for food. Each home I visited seemed to need almost everything, so I always returned to the office with a "yes." Actually the social worker at the League didn't need me to explore. All she really needed to do was send the food baskets. I loved the opportunity, however, to visit these people and would have continued if George had not stepped in. He was apparently afraid I would be exposed to colds, flu, or whatever. I think in reality he was worried about my entering the homes of strangers even though in those days it seemed there was no reason to fear. At that time everything George said I should do, I did. It took me a long time to really become my own person.

Chapter Five

I am convinced that the soul is indestructible and that
its activity will continue through eternity. It is like
the sun which to our eyes seems to set at night, but
has in reality only gone to diffuse its light elsewhere.

—*Goethe*

One day early in 1932 one of my growing up friends, who now also lived in Los Angeles, said to me, "Have you ever heard of automatic writing?" I replied in the affirmative and strongly said, "Naomi, it gives me the creeps and I don't even want to talk about it." My friend respected my feelings until one day she asked me to read a paper she had. I wish I had that paper today, for whatever it said changed our lives. It made so much sense to me that I wanted to know immediately who had written it. "It was channeled," she said, "through automatic writing." I decided that the delivery method no longer mattered, for it was the most logical concept about life and death and why we are here than anything to which I had ever been exposed. My first thought was that I must share this knowledge with George. His logical mind would find it as exciting and provocative as I did, but how would I ever explain from whence it came! I knew he would ask and believed he would never accept anything as bizarre as a person sitting down and getting writing from a person on the other side of life. Remember, at that time no one openly discussed such possibilities. Most of us had been reared with a traditional church background. I knew, however, that somehow I had to share this new and exciting knowledge with him. One night shortly after this, we were driving home from a party in a very mellow mood, when I shared the concept of the contents of that paper. He became as excited as I had been. He did indeed ask that question, "Where did you ever get such material?" When I told him, instead of closing the door, he said we must arrange to meet the person through whom such wisdom had come. I called my friend the next day and discovered the channel had just graduated from UCLA as an English major, and her husband was an engineer. We asked for an introduction, which was arranged. They were invited to our apartment, which by then had a living room and one bedroom. We spent a very pleasant evening together. The next morning I telephoned my friend to ask why they didn't tell us more about their special skills. She laughed and said, "Eleanor, they are not performers and do not automatically volunteer their knowledge. You must ask." It seems difficult for me today to believe that there was a time in our lives when we were too shy to ask what we wanted to know. I think often of the teachings of the great master teacher, Jesus, who said,

"Ask and ye shall receive, seek and it will be given to you." I have learned that the Universe or God, if you will, has given us free will and free choice. Nothing is ever inflicted upon us. It comes as a result of our previous actions or by asking and seeking.

We did invite our new acquaintances to visit us again and this time we not only expressed our interest, but asked many, many questions. We soon became good friends and spent almost every Saturday night together while Ruth, the channel, sat with paper and pencil in hand recording words which were channeled through her. She explained that it was like mental telepathy. She merely had the ability to clear her mind and write the words of another through a clear and unencumbered mind, distinguishing another's thoughts from her own. We were fortunate to have good, intelligent people writing through her. Unfortunately, there are those people who endeavor to get in touch with another dimension of life who are doing so for what they can learn about themselves rather than to seek knowledge or real help. I have always said that in the process of evolution, just because one is dead doesn't make one smart. I believe the transition from this physical life to the next dimension of life, often called the spiritual realm, is merely a transition and reconversion of energy. We take no more knowledge with us than that which we had when we died. We learn as we move ahead. If this is true, why would one want to take advice from just anyone on the spiritual realm who wishes to make contact? I believe that in so doing one would be more apt to be hearing from a soul still hovering around the physical plane unable to conceive of another dimension of life. I feel sure if you or I were to die at this moment, we would be more interested in moving ahead rather than to make contact with a physical being who is curious in wanting to know about themselves. This does not mean that there are no individuals on the other side who respond to those seeking knowledge. We were indeed fortunate that our contacts were endeavoring to answer many questions for us about life and death. If one is serious in seeking higher consciousness and wanting to learn, there is a teacher. I believe that is what happened to us.

One day Hal, the husband of our friend, Ruth, asked if we would be interested in continuing with further study of a much more serious nature rather than the Saturday night "conversations." If so, we would change our rather casual Saturday nights to Sunday afternoons, at which time we would be taught as much as we could comprehend. The information would come through a voice channel from a teacher on a plane far beyond the spiritual.

There were seven of us in the group, Hal and Ruth, a college professor and his wife, a young business woman, George and myself. We were told that the information being given to us would be Universal Truths relative to life and especially the purpose and plan of our existence here. We were also told that such information was being divulged to small groups around the world whose members were seeking knowledge about life and the evolution of life. We were one of these groups. To believe that such knowledge was given to us as a "special" group was something I could not understand or contemplate. In later years, however, I think this was probably true for it was not because we were special in any way, but only that we had open minds and were seriously seeking answers to many questions. Once again, "Ask and ye shall receive, seek and it will be given to you" Yes, I do believe in the power of prayer.

Such knowledge as we received is in the hands of many people today, but often in fragments. I believe that we must be able to look at the whole of life and its relationship to the universe of which we are all a part. Of course there is no way for us to know or be able to comprehend the unlimited or unlimitedness of the universe, for in a sense we are still in kindergarten and we cannot comprehend such vastness any more than a kindergartner can understand the subjects of a college student.

I can only relate what I learned and how it affected my life. We were told that the Universal Power, or what we call God, is in every atom and every form of life and that Universal laws function for all of life on this planet as well as for all others. Scientists today tell us there is no limit to the possible numbers of planetary systems. We are also told that while there is life in other planetary systems, planet Earth is the only one in this solar system to sustain life at this time. Other planets in our system have held life and others will do so eventually, which in our sense of time could be millions or even trillions of what we call years away. In the Universal sense, there is no time or space, a concept which, with our limited vision, is difficult to understand.

We were taught that all life operates under Universal laws with no God sitting on high making judgments. Free will and free choice, the law of cause and effect, what we give out comes back to us, and the greatest of all laws, that of love. We were told that every thought, word and deed are recorded. When we were told this many years ago, I laughed at such a concept. I daresay if we humans can store unlimited amounts of information for instant retrieval through computers, maybe what we call God could do so likewise.

Ultimately, in the "Universal computer" every thought, word and deed or every "entry" of each of us is balanced by an experience of the same value. One takes out what one has given. Has not every great master teacher told us that what we give, we receive? Confucius said, "Whatever you do not want done to yourself, do not do unto others." The Hindu religion states. "Do not unto others which to thee would cause pain." The Islam religion says, "No one of you is a believer until he loves his brother as he loves himself." Jesus said, "Whatsoever ye would that men should do to you, do even so to them." These master teachers

are like us, but have traveled further in the evolutionary process, allowing them to tune into Universal law
knowing that the Universal power is not only power, but
it is love and it is compassion—it is the law of gravity,
of all creation of everything known and unknown. It is
balance and harmony. Do we question this as the sun
rises each day and scientists can predict relationships
of galactic functioning with accurate precision? Each of
us is a part of the evolutionary growth, learning in our
own way. We make our own destiny.

We were told that all is one with the Universal power,
yet Universal power is still over all. It is in a sense like
the peak of a triangle connected and a part of everything
within it, but above it. As the individual energies move
forward or progress in knowledge and learning, they add
positive energy to that Universal power. This action is
never ending as every particle, every grain of sand, all
life is always in motion. In other words, life is eternal. As
life moves forward so too does the Universal power, all
being one.

The basic lessons for us on the physical plane
are simple golden rule lessons such as faith, humility, obedience, tolerance, understanding, charity, and
the greatest of all, which is love. These sound so simple, but are very difficult. The only way we can learn
them is by relationships with others and with all life
on this planet. Needless to say, such lessons take eons
and eons to learn. It is little wonder then that when
one meets a saintly person who seems to have learned

these lessons, we often refer to that person as "an old soul." As that person does indeed become perfect in our sense of perfection, it is no longer necessary for him or her to return to this physical environment, but rather continue to evolve on a higher Universal plane far beyond our comprehension or ability to imagine. This may be what we refer to as "heaven." At least it is apparently the beginning of perfection far beyond anything we can conceive—no pain, no conflict, no limitation of time and space, free to work on planetary systems. I have often thought, although no one, including our teacher, has ever told me, that somewhere in the progress of individual souls, millions join together with their divine love and actually become the sun, having tremendous power to light a planet and give it life. Imagine such a force of love!

We continued these lessons for several years, learning more and more. We learned that some individual souls who have evolved far beyond the physical, choose to help those of us on the physical plane. These are the guardian angels. They stand by and are responsive to our prayers, never inflicting themselves unless asked, obeying the law of free will and free choice. On a very high level of advancement, individuals are given a choice as to whether or not they wish to continue in their evolvement in the Universal work or do so by being reincarnated as a teacher on the physical plane. Few choose the latter, but when they do, they become great spiritual teachers often living obscurely, but not always, perhaps as a Gandhi, a Socrates or Shakespeare. These great teachers instinctively have knowledge far beyond that of the average person, as they are in tune with Universal knowledge to impart to the world. They have chosen to reincarnate as teachers, but in doing so follow the laws which apply to anyone else living a physical life. In other words, the universe does not break its own laws. These teachers, therefore, come back much the same as we do. Their knowledge of Universal laws, their love and compassion assist those of us upon this planet in every way possible, but never inflict themselves upon another or others. We were told that Buddha and Jesus had evolved far, far beyond any others and are truly examples of Universal love and knowledge incarnated here as divine teachers to show us "the way," but the choice is still always ours.

We were told once that humans on this earth cannot truly understand the magnitude of love which is so vast, all encompassing and powerful. The only way I can begin to appreciate a bit of what it must be is the feeling I have when looking at a magnificent sunset, or while walking through a redwood forest, or when witnessing the unlimited beauties of life on our planet. I then try to imagine the love which must have made it all possible, not a human type of love, but a divine power, a force.

When we finally chose to stop and to dwell upon what we had already learned, we had just been given a lesson on the realm of energy wherein highly evolved individual units of souls create, sending the results of their creative efforts on a vibratory wave length to various planets, according to their evolutionary needs. I feel very sure that Thomas Edison's discovery of the way to harness light through the electric light bulb was the capturing of such a creation. Remember Mr. Edison said that he did not know how it worked or from whence this knowledge came. Did you know that just before he died, he was endeavoring to create a machine which would get in touch with another form of life? We were told that nothing is created by individuals on this earth, but received by creative and responsive souls here who, through their own work and efforts, their opening and delving into new possibilities, are able to tune into those vibratory energies and new ideas. People have often remarked upon how often the same idea is presented by two or more individuals at the same time even across the world. New ideas are sent out for a receiver, wherever that may be. This being true, what we call "the creative genius" is one who, by his or her conscientious effort and with what the individual has already learned, is receptive to a higher source of knowledge and energy. This receiving is not usually on a conscious level, but the integrity of the person, the work and the striving for an objective opens the way for the creative forces. This could be an invention, a work of art, a symphony or any number of things which seem to the average among us to be complete genius, and so it is in the highest sense. Beethoven was one of those geniuses who acknowledged that his music came from a higher source. I believe that when one works positively in any field of endeavor with all one's heart and soul, a channel of energy goes into the universe and if one is receptive, a response automatically results.

It was approximately 1934 when we finally stopped pursuing more knowledge, for we knew we had gone as far as we were capable of learning and understanding. It became all too vast for our human minds to comprehend. We were aware, however, that what we had learned would always be a part of us and our lives, aware of the responsibility each of us had to all of life. This knowledge has never ceased to be part of my very being, giving me the assurance that there is no end to life, to love and the light of the Universal power which is within each of us.

Today scientists tell us of our expanding universe and the possibilities of millions of planetary systems all vibrating with Universal energy. The great Einstein said, "Matter can never be destroyed, but can be changed into other forms of energy." Thousands of years ago the Greek philosopher-scientists spoke of the atom in a living universe. To them, the atom was more than a unit of energy. It was also a unit of indestructible consciousness in a continuum of life. Heraclitus (535-475 BC.) said, "The Universe is generated, not according to time, but according to thought." Heraclitus also believed that the soul of man does not die with the body. He saw the universe as a whole, but with constant change and "becoming." Plato said, "Every soul is immortal for whatever is in perpetual motion is immortal." In the 14th Century the Christian thinker Giordano Bruno, executed for his beliefs, said, "When anything dies, we must believe it to be not death, but only change and becoming." How can we set ourselves apart from other human beings who are a part of us, a part of that same Universal energy? We are different from one another even as the stars and the planets, but still part of the whole. I think we have often heard it said that the cell is to the body as the individual is to God or that Universal power. When one cell is not in harmony with others, the body fails to perform with its highest potential. So it is with each other in relationship to all others. We must then be in harmony with one another not only for ourselves, but for the health of our small and magnificent planet and the universe itself. It is like the words of my friend, Kazuko Toyoda, spoken at a world conference in Washington, D.C. in 1988 when she said, "The flutter of a butterfly's wings in Kyoto affects the weather in New York." So too the actions of each individual affects the whole of life in all its forms.

Chapter Six

*Never ever underestimate the power you have
to change the world. Be willing to go to the
place where God intended you to be.*

—Einstein

In addition to our newfound knowledge, 1933
marked a great change in the political and social life
of this country and hence the world. Franklin Delano
Roosevelt became the thirty-second President of the
United States, a time of complete joy for those realizing that there must be change, but utter doom for
those who had always liked it the way it "used to be."
George's father was one of the latter, a fine, intelligent lawyer who had been president of the Board of
Education in Salt Lake City for many years, and a
staunch Republican. I state this for in no way do I wish
to offend those who did not go along with a drastic
change and need to restructure our social system. My
own parents were Republicans, too. I guess this is why
I voted for Herbert Hoover when I became eligible to
vote, still wanting to please my parents as the little girl
I used to be. Immediately after Roosevelt's election,

however, I realized the need and the satisfaction in independent political thinking and thereafter support-ed him completely.

From the day Roosevelt ordered the banks closed as literally a "cooling off" period to help stabilize the economy and teach us the world had not collapsed, it seemed there was an overwhelming desire to sup-port new concepts for social change. There was hope in abundance for those of us who were not tied to the past.

As I look upon those years, I realize more and more that Mrs. Roosevelt had as much influence on the future of this country as the President. Above all, she wanted women to take the leadership in the movement to abolish war. I believe this remarkable woman had the ear of her husband when he said, "The new order of things should reflect not only the ability and brains of our men, but the understanding heart of women." Mrs. Roosevelt did not expect much from men when it came to the manifestation of a will for peace. She stat-ed, "Only women and youth of any country can initiate this change. They will have men to help them later on in the fight, but they will meet some of the same unbe-lief and lethargy that they have come up against in the past."

Eleanor Roosevelt had her own concept of Utopia, where every individual had an income adequate to pro-vide families with ordinary comforts and the pleasures of life, with no incomes so staggeringly large that he or she did not have to think about expenditures. Such a community, she felt, would have the germs of a really new deal for the race. She believed the depression was caused as much by defects of spirit and character as by institutions. Selfishness and a preoccupation with material things had been the hallmark of the decade. In the frenzy to make money, Americans had lost some of the qualities that made life worthwhile—the ability to enjoy simple things, a landscape, the scent of a rose, the wild creatures of land and sea, and above all, the joy of sharing with one another. She stressed the fact that one part of the country or group cannot prosper while others go without basic needs, and that one country cannot go on gaily while the rest of the world is suffering. She said, "If our country does just the temporary and expedient things, we will find ourselves again where we are today still building a civilization on human suffering." She knew that recovering from the depression would be a time of distress, but also a time when men and women might be more disposed than usual to subordinate selfishness and private interests to common needs. She warned against a return to the "old way." How sad that we did not listen to this very wise and compassionate woman!

Soon after President Roosevelt was elected, he proposed a New Deal for our country. Among other things, the New Deal brought about Social Security, increased the right of employees to bargain, introduced legislation to protect small businesses, and introduced legislation to repeal Prohibition. It was indeed tragic for our nation that we ever had the 18th Amendment, for it taught us how to break the law of the land. What were called "Speakeasies" were opened, wherein one could knock on a door in an alley or other obscure place, enter and order alcoholic drinks. Many citizens learned for the first time how to break the law. In doing so we gave birth to what would later be called the Mafia, law breakers and dealers in dope of all kinds. It is my opinion that we should make the use of marijuana as available as alcohol and cigarettes thus breaking a long line of arrests and illegal distributors. The law of "Three Strikes" is placing people in our prisons who should have treatment and education rather than incarceration, which is a breeding ground for hate, fear and, ultimately, terrorism.

Our nation was not the only one to benefit from the New Deal, for George and I had our own "New Deal." One day George was asked if he might be interested in a position at 20th Century-Fox Film Corporation and was told by the head of the studio, Mr. Winfield Sheehan, that he had heard that George was one of the best young trial lawyers in Los Angeles. Of course George was interested. After meeting with Mr. Sheehan, however, George learned that the position didn't pay any more than he was receiving. It didn't take long in their conversations for Mr. Sheehan to raise the salary. George still said "no." Finally, Mr. Sheehan raised it again, so George said he would take the position for one year. When George's first pay check arrived, we learned that Mr. Sheehan had been talking about a weekly salary and George thought it was a monthly one. Just four years out of college and during the depression, George and I felt we were no less than millionaires. Instead of staying for one year, George stayed twenty. That was our "New Deal."

The following years were very happy ones for us. We moved from the heart of the city to a lovely studio apartment in Beverly Hills, so George could be near his office. This, incidentally, was in the administration building with all the other executives of the corporation. At that time it was a small building, in contrast to the one today which is a block long. The Fox lot covered 300 acres. Much of this land today is Century City. In those days the Hollywood stars were signed to a contract with one of the studios: 20th Century-Fox, United Artists, Paramount, Universal and Metro Goldwyn Mayer. Stars would then be contracted out to another studio as so much merchandise, with approval from the actor as well as the studio, primarily the latter. George was responsible for all these contract agreements. In fact, even though he was employed because of his successful court work, in all the years he was there, he only tried one lawsuit, which he won.

At the conclusion of each film the studio had a party to celebrate. We met in the studio commissary, where champagne and huge bowls of caviar were served. Among the stars under contract to Fox in those days were Shirley Temple, Alice Faye, Judy Garland, Tyrone Power, Warner Baxter, Janet Gaynor, and Will Rogers. Others who appeared through the trade agreements were Clark Gable, Joan Crawford, Fred Astaire, Ginger Rogers and many others. I remember the first time Marilyn Monroe danced before a small audience at the studio prior to her ever being in a film. She was very young and had just been signed up as a pretty girl with possible talent. No one could have dreamed she would become a legend.

Chapter Seven

Our task must be to widen our circle of
compassion to embrace all living creatures
and the whole of nature in its beauty.

—Albert Einstein

In 1935, our lives took a new direction. I became
pregnant, as we had hoped I would. George and I sought
out the best obstetrician we could find, who happened to
be a rather pompous old gentleman. After the examina-
tion, which brought us the confirmation we had hoped
for, George stated that, as a partner in this wonderful
experience, we had agreed that he should be present
at the birth of this child. The doctor raised an eyebrow
and said, "I really do not think this will be necessary,
for I have never lost a father yet." George stood up and
said, "I am sorry, doctor, but you have just lost one." I
was a bit embarrassed, never wanting to ruffle feathers,
but proud of George's stand. We found a marvelous doctor who also became our friend and was happy to have
George share this miracle of birth.

On August 10, 1935 Dianne arrived. This day
brought George and me overwhelming joy. It was also a

45

day of deep sorrow, for our beloved friend, philosopher and actor, Will Rogers, was killed as he and Wiley Post were flying on a peace mission. Shortly before Rogers left, he had asked George to become his personal attorney, to which George agreed, planning to leave Fox and the corporation work he was doing. George stayed at Fox, however, for another seventeen years.

During my pregnancy with Dianne, I had some reservations and indeed some fears. They were not about the actual birth, but about the lifelong responsibilities, physically and mentally. The only thing I knew about motherhood I learned from my mother, whom I adored. While my mother did everything possible to make our wedding the magnificent one it was, I did not realize until I moved away to California that the loss she felt in our companionship and her ability to live vicariously through me were so deep that she became an extremely unhappy woman. My father's love did not fill the void. The fact that she was suffering from pernicious anemia, which at the time we did not know, contributed to her depression. I began saying to myself that if this is what having children does to a parent, I am not sure I can handle it. I then decided the way to do so would be to make my children completely independent from the onset. Much to the psychological distress of my lovely daughter, Dianne, I did just this. I nursed her for only a few weeks and taught her how to drink from a cup when she was only nine months old. Every indication of her growth and advancement meant success for me as a mother with an independent child. The fact that she began sucking her thumb at an early age did not tell me that she had been deprived of nursing and the sucking instinct. How unfortunate that the few psychology courses I had taken had not taught me a thing about motherhood. What a pity it is too that one of the most important functions in life is scarcely mentioned in our educational system! By the time Dianne was taking her first steps, I had learned the joys and delights of being a parent and knew I wanted more children. I learned much, much later that my early behavior left an imprint upon Dianne, which was never quite erased until life provided an opportunity to share our feelings and to provide the healing which is one of my most precious gifts.

The pleasure Dianne brought to us made us know that we wanted at least three more children, even though we had to settle for two. Joan came along on Flag Day, June 14, 1938. With an expanded family, we moved into a ten-room house on North Hillcrest Road in Beverly Hills. Life was abundantly happy, for George and I were completely in love, proud and happy with our children. We lived in a lovely English home with a beautiful garden, we had a cook, a governess, friends and freedom to do whatever we wished. George continued to enjoy his work, which gave him personal satisfactions and money enough to be free from financial worries. In addition to enjoying the children, I continued to take classes at UCLA. I enjoyed friends during the day and small dinner parties at night. I read a bit and led a relaxed life, which

I see some people doing today and I ask myself "where is their conscience?" If it had not been for the state of the world and our involvement in World War II, I wonder if I would ever have awakened. While the early spiritual teachings we received helped me in many ways, my personal life was so secure and happy that I sailed on my own cloud, asleep for a while.

Rumblings of war were emerging in the late 1930s. The signing of the Versailles Treaty left Germany in poverty with no promise of assistance or emergence from the devastation of four long years of war. The country became ripe for leadership and promises of recovery, and so it was that the voice of Adolph Hitler gained power and the people listened. If only there had been compassion, instead of condemnation, perhaps there would never have been a Hitler.

I shall never forget the first time I heard the voice of this man. It was shortly after the Germans had invaded Czechoslovakia. The screaming power and hatred in his voice, and the reaction of thousands of German troops in a state of hypnotized idolatry, were blood chilling and aroused our consciousness to the fact that hate was rampant in the world. From that moment on, we knew we could not escape the fact that the world is one and, much as we wanted to believe that we were separated by the Atlantic Ocean, the fumes of war were coming nearer to our shores. Ignoring this fact, however, was a policy in which we wanted to indulge and did so for several years until Germany's ally, Japan, forced us into a declaration of war.

Chapter Seven

Early in 1940, George and I decided to learn to fly. It was something both of us had wanted to do, but now with possible war over the horizon, we had a reason in addition to the pleasure and satisfaction of fulfilling a desire. We knew that if the United States were drawn into a war, we were too old (in our early thirties) to be recruited, but we might be able to help in some way by ferrying planes, which surely would be needed. As it happened, we later discovered that twenty-six was the cut-off age for such endeavors for non-enlisted personnel. But both of us agreed that learning to fly and flying itself was one of the most exciting and stimulating experiences we had ever had, so we continued. We signed up for a flying lesson each morning at sunrise or late afternoon, before or after George was at work. This did not mean we flew every day, for California fog prevented the clear visibility needed for flying in an open cockpit plane with no instruments. Nothing but flying had any claim on our time except a sick child or an office emergency. We flew for little over a year until the bombing of Pearl Harbor, when all non-military planes were forbidden on the west coast. Among those learning to fly with us were such Hollywood stars as Jimmy Stewart, Olivia DeHaviland, and my good friend until his early death, Tyrone Power.

Our flying instructor was written up in one of the national magazines as "the toughest and best teacher in the country." He certainly was the former, demanding utmost perfection, always reminding us that one cannot walk away from a mistake in flying. He was also a most personable man, redheaded, handsome and lovable especially when he was not swearing at one of us through the gasport when we failed to comply with his instructions. I shall never forget the day I first saw him walking across the field with his parachute thrown across his back. I thought he was one of the most beautiful men I had ever seen. I was in love without ever knowing that he was to be our instructor. What do we do when we meet someone with whom we have been in love in another existence? This was difficult for me, for George was my first and only love, but still I loved this man too. We later learned that we both loved one another and expressed this love. I have always had a certain amount of guilt even though it seems natural that when one loves in one lifetime, why should it terminate when one meets in another? With the declaration of war our instructor became a commander in the navy and flew planes from the U.S. to the Soviet Union. I saw him only once thereafter. We declared our love for one another, but we knew it had terminated—at least in this existence.

In the summer of 1941 it seemed ever more inevitable that war was something our country could not avoid, even though we never dreamed we would be attacked. Realizing or believing there would be an increased need for trained nurses abroad, thus depleting the supply at home, the American Red Cross issued a statement in the Los Angeles Times asking for volunteers to take an intensive training course for nurse's aides. Having a governess at home for the girls, and with George's approval, my friend, Lois Wilson, a former actress in the early days of films, and I applied. We were told that only twenty would be accepted. We waited three months before we learned that we were two of them. Our classes were three days a week and taught by the former Director of the School of Nurses at Stanford University. She assured us we would be called upon to do more than empty bed pans, bathe and make beds, so we were taught to take blood and handle minor wounds, a practice later discouraged for the classes which followed ours. After several months we "graduated' and were assigned to the only hospital in Los Angeles which would accept volunteers, the Children's Orthopedic Hospital. We all felt the staff there was not too worried about us, for most of the children were in full body casts, so we couldn't really get "too close" to them to do any damage. We had to be on duty at 6:00 a.m., ready for a six-hour shift. We carried our starched uniforms across town and changed at the hospital so we would be "germ free" for our duties, which we took very seriously and not without some pride. I doubt that there were many women in those days who had not at some time hoped to become a nurse. After all, it was one of the few professions where women were welcomed.

Chapter Eight

We must all learn to live together as brothers
and sisters or we will perish together as fools.
—Martin Luther King, Jr.

December 7, 1941 is a date anyone in America who was alive then will always remember. News came to us on a bright, sunny Sunday morning that Pearl Harbor had been bombed. We were paralyzed and in a state of total disbelief. The days which followed included hearing the voice of President Roosevelt declaring war, and were filled with tears, fears, uncertainties and confusion. Despite the fact that we were at war, there was a new kind of strength and dedication on the part of everyone. We were no longer thinking of ourselves, but doing everything we could to support the war effort. How sad that it takes such a catastrophe to arouse the individual spirit and move us into action. As with any war, we had an "enemy" and this time one we could identify because of the shape of their eyes and the color of their skin. I was as guilty as anyone, not knowing which was a "real" American and which was still a "Japanese" waiting to kill us. What a dreadful and despicable thing it was to round up all the Japanese in our country, confiscate everything they owned and then place them and their children in camps far from cities and everything they knew. War immediately robs us of our sanity and our compassion. So it did early in 1942 when many of our friends were doomed to a desolate life behind barbed wire fences for the remainder of the war years.

Although we "won" that war, there are many things in our society today resulting from the things we did and the things we learned through the billions of dollars spent on "winning" this war. The first thing we learned was how to produce weapons of death by mass production, an "art" still in progress as we allocate billions of dollars today to do just this. We developed deadly chemicals, many of which are used now to kill insects and produce eye appealing fruits and vegetables, destroying the biological nature of the earth which I believe is affecting the health of people in a sinister and unseen way.

During those years each of us worked in the best way we knew. George became an air-raid warden. Men from each block throughout the city volunteered to patrol at night watching for unseen action and to help in case of bombings, which we truly believed to be a possibility. We only had two very scary nights when unidentified objects were believed to be spotted. This resulted in a complete blackout and the only time I could even begin to identify with the people in England and Europe, and later Japan, thinking of a bomb dropping on my children and snuffing out the lives of countless individuals.

Three days a week or more I volunteered as a nurse's aide. Four of us were selected from that first class to help the doctors and nurses open a blood bank, the first of its kind in the United States. We were all in this together, for even the professionals did not know how to establish such a unit involving the general public standing in line to offer their blood. In addition to working at the blood center, we went to the ship-building yards in San Pedro to take the offer of blood from the shipbuilders. They were turning out ships daily following one pattern, so mass production became a special skill, the like of which had never been attempted before. I have often said that the people who were rejected for military services because of physical or mental limitations went into construction jobs such as building ships and planes. When the war ended, these people were the first to be discharged and took their well earned savings and bought property, had one design and then built millions and millions, row upon row of houses in the same kind of mass production skills they had used to build ships. No originality or diversity, an eyesore today to the landscapes of this nation.

The greatest horror to come from the war, of course, was the building of the atomic bomb used for the purpose of reigning death and destruction upon our adversaries. How totally tragic that we have used the gifts from the universe to kill rather than bring power and light to the world. Even David Lilienthal, the first Chairman of the Atomic Energy Commission, said that had we have waited, we could have developed atomic energy without the use of plutonium and the destructive waste products. Only fear can produce such negative actions.

After the war, I hung up my nurse's aide uniform and turned my concerns to the community and the recently formed United Nations, which we believed to be the hope of our future. I still feel it has been a tremendous power for good throughout the world with the potential for an ever greater organization still before us.

About this time I became President of the Hawthorne School P.T.A., a position I turned down flatly until my mother stepped in. She was visiting us the day I was asked to take this position. When I said I would not do it, my mother said, "Eleanor, I have heard you criticize this organization. I do not think you have a right to criticize anything if you are not willing to do something to make it better." This is why I acquiesced and took the job. It was probably one of the best things I ever did, for I learned to stand before an audience and express myself as well as to begin to learn the meaning of a leadership role. One of the highlights resulting from that year was the organization of the Beverly

Hills Community Forum. It was developed in order to educate the community relative to the structure of the United Nations and its various agencies such as World Health, UNESCO, etc. My George was elected chairman of the sessions. Dr. Dean McHenry, Dean of the School of Political Science at UCLA, became the moderator. Interestingly enough, Dr. McHenry later became the Chancellor of the University of California at Santa Cruz and had a major role in designing this magnificent campus with its ten colleges in the midst of giant redwood forests, very near my present home.

Speaking of homes, shortly after the advent of war, we moved into a charming house on Alpine Drive, a block from the children's school and something I could manage, as all the household help had moved into the defense industries and beyond. It was there that I first met Marjorie Fasman. Marjorie and I have worked harmoniously together for over fifty years. Her intelligence, her humor, compassion and creative genius have added immeasurably to the joys and satisfactions of my life all along the way. One of the first projects we undertook together was saving the trees in Beverly Hills. We didn't know why the beautiful trees throughout the city were being cut down and replaced by very young ones. We became weekly visitors at the City Hall questioning, protesting and ultimately discovering that the head of the Parks and Recreation Department for the city also owned the nursery that was selling the city the replacement trees. His business thrived until we appeared. I still look with pride at the many trees lining the streets in Beverly Hills because we cared enough to save many of them. Too few of us, I fear, remember that every single idea in the history of the world began in the mind of one person. What that person did or does with the idea is all that matters. Nothing is achieved if we do not act.

The next project in which Marjorie and I were involved was heading up the Community Chest Drive (now United Way). Once again we did not like what we saw. We felt Beverly Hills could raise more money than it was doing if we changed the way we were doing it and made fundraising fun. Our voices were heard, which resulted in our being asked to be chairmen of the next drive. We could see no reason why a door-to-door canvas should go on for three months when it could be done in one day with advance and proper planning and good use of the media. The first thing we did was to approach the owner of an empty storefront on Wilshire Boulevard next to Saks Fifth Avenue to donate the space, which he did. We then went to the prop department at one of the major studios and secured beautiful rugs and furnishings. We hung a huge Red Feather flag, the symbol of the campaign, over the entrance so everyone on Wilshire Boulevard would know we were in the business of raising funds for good causes. We didn't believe that any group working to raise funds for the total community should be in a little office on the third floor, as was the custom then.

We wanted the community to know we were there. Our plan was to get 1,000 volunteers to give only three hours on what we called "C" Day. Prior to this day, Marjorie and I, with one of my flying companions, flew over the city dropping flyers announcing the event. We spent much time on press and radio, so when "C' Day actually arrived, people were prepared to give their dollars. Packets were ready for the first team, which worked from 9:00 a.m. to noon. They rang doorbells and asked for contributions from all people listed in their packet, and returned with money and packets to the office. The office team then removed the money and names of those who had given, and by one o'clock they were ready for the next team. This continued throughout the day with new teams taking over. By nine o'clock that night almost every household in Beverly Hills had been reached, with an increase of over 150% in giving from the year before. Of course, this took good organization and planning, but everyone had fun. Follow-up crews were sent out during the next few days to reach those businesses and any others who had not been solicited.

Shortly after the end of the Second World War, training was given to a small group at UCLA designed to help educate soldiers and civilians relative to our abilities to come together with greater understanding. Our lives as civilians were in total contrast to those of our troops, who were in battle living with death and destruction while we were at home in comparative comfort and ease. As a result of that UCLA instruction,

two of us were invited to the Veteran's Administration
to develop an educational program for those who were
psychologically damaged as a result of their war experiences. We met with the two under whom we were to
work, Mr. Ben Reinhart and Mr. Francis Marquardt.
They told us we would be teaching in the women's unit
for they were the most difficult to reach. Reach we did,
but not in the manner of developing an educational
program, which was the request. We soon learned that
these patients were not ready to listen to lectures or to
learn, so we decided to arouse their interest through
music. With the approval of "our bosses," we brought a
songwriter out to play for these patients and talk about
the songs he had written. They were not interested in
listening, but they did respond to the music and some
even danced with one another. Realizing education was
not in the realm of awakening these patients, we had
another idea. Virginia, my friend and co-worker, decided to go to Romanoff's restaurant in Beverly Hills. At
that time, this was "the" restaurant where Hollywood's
elite gathered for luncheon. We cornered several of
our friends including Cesar Romero, Reginald Denny,
Tyrone Power, Leon Ames, and others, all important
Hollywood stars at the time. We asked them if they
would be willing to go to the Veterans' Administration
every Tuesday afternoon when they were not making
a film to dance with these psychologically disturbed
patients who had recently returned from the war.
Without exception they said they would. Phone calls to

other male stars brought out quite a contingent. After calls to members of one of the best bands, we had a dance. Our psychology was that if important people were willing to come out to see these patients, it would boost their morale. Not many weeks into the program, instead of sitting around in robes looking disheveled, patients began going to the ward beautician to get their hair done. They dressed, they danced, and some of them, with the help of their doctors began to get well. One day I asked Reginald Denny, a stage and screen star of many years ago, how Rosie, his favorite patient, was getting along. He replied by saying, "Fine, she no longer talks about sewing buttons on ice cream cones."

This program continued for several years and I can truly say it was one of the most gratifying projects in which I was ever involved. Commendations came to us from the chief medical officer, who assured us that we had truly made a difference in the lives of these patients. I do believe we were able to open doors for them to receive the professional help they needed.

1915 Mollie Dalrymple
and John W. Walsh,
Eleanor's parents.

1930 Eleanor and George with
their new Ford Cabriolet,
costing $800.

1940 Eleanor in one
of the planes she flew
called a Fleet.

1941 Eleanor with
her young daughters.

1945 Eleanor and
her husband, George,
in their Beverly Hills home.

1945 Joan, Eleanor and Dianne
at home on Alpine Drive,
Beverly Hills.

1948 Eleanor with the actor, Cesar Romero when he volunteered to help with the Community Chest Drive.

1948 Eleanor, Marjorie Fasman with pilot, Max Stanley.

1948 Marjorie Fasman, the Mayor of Beverly Hills and Eleanor on a fire truck on Wilshire Boulevard during a campaign.

1949 The Mayor of Beverly Hills presenting Eleanor with an Award for her volunteer leadership with her friend Helen Guggenheim.

1962 Dr. Stafford Warren, founding Dean, UCLA School of Medicine prior to his leaving for Washington D.C. to join President Kennedy's cabinet, with Eleanor.

1972 Actor John Forsythe as he presented Eleanor with the UCLA Award for Distinguished Service.

1981 Eleanor sitting on the Great Wall of China.

1984 Eleanor with Margaret Bell, then President of IAVE, with Japanese Prince Mikasa.

1985 The opera singer and actress, Dorothy Kirsten French, Eleanor and actress and philanthropist Helen Hays.

1987 Eleanor in Yalta during days of Soviet Union.

1987 Eleanor at Yalta in front of the palace where the World War II Peace Treaty was signed.

1990 Max Smith, son in-law, Eleanor and Joan the day she received her doctoral degree.

1990 Eleanor at home in Santa Cruz, California.

1992 Dr. Hana Nasir, President BirZeit University, East Palestine with Eleanor.

1992 Eleanor standing, second from the right, with Israeli and Palestinian "Women in Black for Peace" in West Jerusalem.

1993 Celeste Holm and Eleanor at Sundance.

1995 Eleanor with Thich Nhat Hanh's assistant, Sister Chan Khong at the "State of the World Forum," San Francisco.

1996 John Robbins, Eleanor and Robert Kennedy Jr.

1997 Dr. Helen Caldicott and Eleanor.

2002 Eleanor's daughters, Dianne Wright and Joan Smith.

2002 Mayor's Proclamation, Santa Cruz.

2004 Eleanor with singer and composer, Terry Bradford.

Chapter Nine

The only ones among you who will be truly happy are those who will have sought and found how to serve.

—Albert Schweitzer

In 1947 I became the President of the Los Angeles Mental Hygiene Society. Once again our job was to educate. Our speakers included Governor Earl Warren, later to become Chief Justice of the U.S. Supreme Court responsible for the Roe vs. Wade decision relative to abortion rights. Dr. Benjamin Spock was another renowned author who stayed at our home when he came to speak. I wish I had known him when our children were tiny. He was the first in my era to recommend feeding babies when they were hungry instead of on the every four hour routine as young mothers were taught. I so well remember waiting for that last five minutes before picking up my children to feed them even though they had been wailing from hunger. Dr. Spock also advocated a meatless and dairyless diet for all people. He continued until his death in 1997 to receive resistance to his ideas and his vision.

As a result of my work with the Mental Hygiene Society, I was appointed by Governor Earl Warren to become a member of the first California Commission on Mental Health. I was one of twenty, along with Dr. Stafford Warren, who had been recently appointed Dean of the yet to be built UCLA School of Medicine. Dr. Warren was responsible for a total change in my life, leading to a career for which I shall always be grateful. Members of this Commission met every month in Sacramento at the State Capitol Building. We made a number of recommendations still to be implemented and this was back in the late 1940s. Among them was making it mandatory for large businesses to provide mental health counseling, as well as child care centers for their employees. We were eager to provide services for many of the mentally and emotionally ill before illness became chronic, and to provide services for the benefit of both children and adults, creating a more healthy society. This is once again a reminder that evolution moves very slowly. I need to remind myself of this more and more as I see the turmoil in much of the world growing from old wounds festering into angers and hatreds and ultimately war. I believe that until the needs of all creatures are met, we can never have peace.

As I was taking leadership roles, so was George. He became President of the United Nations Association in Los Angeles, along with his many responsibilities at the studio. We always had time, however, to be with one another and the children in the evening and I always managed to be home by the time school was out in the afternoon. Not so long ago I was happy to hear my Joan state that she was happy that I was always there in the afternoon when she and Dianne returned from school.

The Los Angeles Volunteer Bureau had always been of interest to me. In 1950 I became its third president. The concept of having an organization for the specific purpose of matching volunteers wanting to serve with the needs in the community was entirely new. Evelyn Davis was its Director, a great and beloved lady. She was beautiful and compassionate. She taught me one of the best lessons I have ever had by her own example. I watched her plant ideas in other's heads, then help nurture them and give the credit to that person. She knew the result of an idea is all that is important, not who gets the credit. She gave credit to many of us young women for what had been her ideas, never making us aware of this, but building up our own belief in our ability to make change. Later I learned what a joy it is to give inspiration and strength to others helping them to become achievers.

During those days when Dr. Warren and I were flying back and forth to Sacramento, he spoke of wanting me to organize the volunteer and auxiliary programs at the UCLA Medical Center, later to become known as the UCLA Center for Health Sciences. I was not too enthusiastic and said to Dr. Warren, "I am not quite sure I would want to work solely with a group of women." Not that I disliked women, heavens no! It was just that I always liked the idea of differing opinions and approaches. Remember at that time all volunteers in hospitals were women, mostly those whose children had grown. How that pattern has changed! In 1954, he asked me again, Dr. Warren was a tall and handsome man, gentle but powerful. He always seemed to have a smile on his face which seemed to say, "You just wait." When he asked me again, I felt honored. I had watched this building grow from a hole in the ground to the largest building west of the Mississippi. There was a hospital and clinics to serve the patients, research laboratories, a School of Nursing, Public Health with Dentistry and a Psychiatric Institute in the planning.

Early in 1955, I gathered together thirty community leaders including several wives of the medical staff and Vi Warren, the Dean's delightful wife. We went to work planning a volunteer service department and an auxiliary for fundraising. Like most everything else at the University of California, our plans had to be approved by Members of the Board of Regents. This they did with one exception. There must be a full time department head, a Coordinator of Volunteers Services. At that time this was a budding profession with only three directors in all Los Angeles and few throughout the country. One day over tea Vi Warren said, "Whatever are we going to do to find a Director of Volunteers?" I said I had no idea, but whoever it would be would be the most fortunate woman in the world. She seemed surprised and urged me to apply. I was amazed, for I had never held a position nor did I have a degree. Even though I had never stopped taking classes, I never followed the curriculum leading to a degree, but took those classes which interested me most. While I am a member of the class of '30 at UCLA and listed as a graduate in the Alumni Bulletin, I still need more required units to graduate. I plan to do this in my next existence. In addition, I had to discuss such a possibility with George. This remarkably wonderful man was always totally supportive of any activity in which I was interested. By this time the girls were grown. Dianne was married and Joan was away at Bishop School in La Jolla, so a full-time job would be possible.

After receiving George's blessing, I made a date with Mildred Foreman, the Personnel Director at UCLA. I told her of my interest and a bit about my volunteer activities. I hastened to state that I was being rather presumptuous applying for a position at the University when I didn't even have a degree. I could have hugged her on the spot when she replied very casually by saying, "What has that to do with it?" I was quite sure when we parted that the position would be mine. I then hastened to call Evelyn Davis, for I still doubted my ability to assume such a position. As always she gave me great support and encouragement. Soon I learned that the position was really mine, to begin officially in October of 1955.

Now it was September with a huge job in front of me. I was still acting chairperson for the newly formed UCLA Medical Center Auxiliary. On September 22 we would be presenting the plans to the community at a large luncheon in the ballroom of the newly opened Beverly Hilton Hotel, the first big event to take place there. This was one of the events of the season with headlines in the L.A. Press. The President of the University of California, Robert Sproul, with the UCLA Chancellor and other local celebrities attended. My friend, Marjorie Fasman, with her creative genius, utilized the architect's blueprints for the centerpieces. In those days they were truly "Blue Prints," beautiful blue paper with plans for the Auxiliary drawn on each one. What a change the computer world has brought to this field as in most others today.

This event was my last community volunteer venture for the next twenty years, for on October 6, 1955 I signed University of California papers as the University's first Coordinator of Volunteer Services. I could not be called a "Director" at that time, for this title was reserved for the academic staff only. I did become a department head, however, serving under the Administrator of the Hospital. Mr. Kenneth Eastman. He was never quite sure what I was supposed to do. At that time I doubt that even the American Hospital Association had a job description for a Director of Volunteer Services. This made my job extremely pleasant for I felt no restrictions and was free to move ahead with the Dean of the School of the Medicine believing so completely in the power and effectiveness of volunteers. He also believed there must be ample space for a volunteer program which could become one of the largest departments at the center in terms of numbers of people. I had been given a very small office, but Dr. Warren changed this. He took me into a magnificent suite off the main lobby. There was a huge room which I learned would be my office, a conference room, a kitchen, restrooms and ample cupboard space with a glassed-in area which Dr. Warren assured me would one day be an Auxiliary Gift Shop, which ultimately it was. Of course, I was overwhelmed by such luxurious space, for even the hospital administrator had nothing like this. Dr. Warren was truly a visionary man, for all he had dreamed came true. He told me that he had always believed that volunteers are the lifeline between an institution and the community which they serve, bringing skills, interest and time, taking back into the community knowledge of the institution and how it functions. He went so far as to say he believed the staff performs even better when a volunteer is there. He said it is like having a guest for dinner—we seem to put our house in better order. I asked him how he managed to have such quarters designed. Surely in the eyes of the Regents and architects, volunteers at that time did not seem that important. Stafford Warren, in addition to being a brilliant, warm and loving man, was a politician and a diplomat. He was later appointed by

President Kennedy to become a member of his Cabinet. His political ingenuity had everything to do with our having that space. Early on when the plans for the building were being designed, he said it might be nice if the Regents would care to have their monthly meetings at the Medical Center, so space was drawn in by the architects. The Regents did indeed have one meeting there shortly after the building opened, but decided not to meet there again. I don't doubt that my beloved Stafford Warren had hoped from the beginning what the end result would be. Thanks to the wisdom of this great man and the space he provided, we were able to develop one of the finest volunteer programs in the country with up to 3,000 volunteers, young, old, male and female, working in the hospital and clinics, and in the many research laboratories and offices. During the twenty years I was at the university I was given many opportunities to grow and to learn. I was fortunate being a pioneer in a new field of endeavor involving giving people. As the years went by, more and more hospitals were employing volunteer directors, so we organized in order to share and to learn. I then became the first President of the Southern California Society of Directors of Volunteer Services, later holding the same position with the American Hospital Association. I was often asked to be a faculty member. I was invited to speak at the California, Western, and American Hospital Association Conventions and Workshops, taking me throughout the United States and Hawaii before it became a state, meeting wonderful people and learning from them. During the sixties I served as Chairperson of the UCLA Policy Commission. This was established at the same time students were demanding a voice in campus policies. I was glad my term was for only one year, for I felt no sense of accomplishment there. Later, I received the UCLA Distinguished Service Award. I doubt that it was for that effort, however.

The most precious gift of the many gifts which came to me during those years was the privilege of working with the volunteers. I learned early on that most people have so much more ability than they think they have, especially women. I cannot tell you the countless times during an interview of hearing a woman say, "I want to help in some way, but I haven't any special skills for I am just a housewife. "Just a housewife!" How much we have all learned as housewives in flexibility, love, humor, patience, listening, and the myriad of skills which deal with family and community living, all those attributes most needed in a health science center, in fact throughout life.

There wasn't much money in the university budget for the volunteer program, so my staff was limited to one assistant. We also needed someone friendly and capable at the front desk every day from 8:00 to 5:00. We soon found five remarkable women willing to give that time in order to greet visitors, welcome regular and perspective volunteers, help to schedule and assign. Typing was an added plus, a skill they all had.

This left us free for interviewing, working with staff, designing new jobs in areas wherein volunteer help could upgrade a whole service and of course educating and orienting. I have always said a successful volunteer director, like a housewife, must be able to do many things at one time with and for people in an atmosphere constantly in motion. I must say here that when I retired at the end of twenty years, those five volunteers who held down the front desk were still there and continued to work with many others who had been given positions of responsibility. We all need to be needed and these volunteers knew they were.

During the years from 1948 to 1952, television was moving from the research laboratories to a reality in homes across America. Not only did we hear voices, but we saw pictures! How can anyone believe that space is not filled with energy? How else could sound and pictures be transmitted except by reconverting energy from the sender to the receiver? What a magical world! I well remember the first television set, which was contributed by a generous donor to the children in the pediatrics unit shortly after I began working there. Most of such gifts came through our office. I accepted it with great joy, as did the children. The next morning the hospital superintendent came into my office with a university rule book. He said, "It says here in rule #17 that any gift coming to the University of California must be accepted by the Regents prior to actual acceptance." I was aghast and called my mentor, Dr. Warren.

He of course laughed and said. "Eleanor, as long as you are here, use your own judgment and do anything you wish as long as it does not hurt anyone." I not only followed his advice, but decided that rules are made for morons.

In addition to the success of the volunteer program, the Auxiliary continued to thrive under the leadership of its first President, Anita Louise, a Hollywood actress and wife of the President of 20th Century-Fox Film Corporation. This was a coup for the Auxiliary as money raising was its primary objective, supplying extra needs and services for patients which the university, being a teaching institution, did not provide. The first fundraiser was the premiere of the film, "The King and I," which netted $25,000, a tremendous sum for the year 1956. Many events led up to the night of the premiere. One of which I well remember included the bringing together of the nation's most glamorous stars, who sang for the patients. One of them was the legendary Metropolitan Opera star, Dorothy Kirsten, who later became a very important part of my life as we shared our common joys and sorrows.

By this time, as I mentioned earlier, our daughters were grown and away. Our Dianne, who married rather young, was living in Manhattan Beach with her husband, Harlan Wright, a biomedical engineer. They were married in All Saints', our family church in Beverly Hills where Joan and her Max, now a prominent architect, were later to be married. Even though we were not churchgoers, All Saints' was truly our family church because the Dean of Rowland Hall, where I went to high school, became the minister of All Saints' when he left Salt Lake City the day after George's and my wedding. We loved him and he loved us. Joan was busy in a leadership role at Bishop's School in La Jolla, a sister school to Rowland Hall. She was always taking care of someone needing a listening ear. She later earned a doctoral degree in social sciences and eventually became the Director of The National Conference of Community and Justice in Salt Lake City. With both girls away, George and I were alone sharing a new kind of romance. George had left the studio in 1952 and opened law offices in Beverly Hills. He drove me to work each day and picked me up at night. It was marvelous sharing together as we did. The evenings were spent with total joy as we stopped at our favorite restaurants on our way home or went on to enjoy martinis and dinner in our beautiful little Santa Monica Canyon home overlooking the ocean, which we bought in 1962.

Chapter Ten

Our lives begin to end the day we become
silent about the things that matter.

—Martin Luther King, Jr.

At this time the scientific world was moving far afield and in 1957 the Soviet Union put a man into space. This was just a little over half a century from the first flight of the Wright Brothers in 1903. Not long after this great achievement by the Russians, our beloved young president, John Fitzgerald Kennedy, told us we would be the first to put a man on the moon— and so we were! I have often wondered what the world would have been like if this caring man had lived. Little did he, nor any of us, dream when he achieved the signing of the Test Ban Treaty in 1963 that we would go on to break it in essence by testing underground and then continuing to build massive weapons of death and destruction. The building of these weapons is still a sickness from which it seems we have not yet recovered. If only humans were wise enough, the trillions spent on weapons could be transferred into the necessities for life, all life. It seems to take so very long for us humans to learn that there is no way to have a positive result from a negative action. Surely, through the ravages of war, we can see that this is true despite the fact that the technologies learned through the war effort have brought other good products which are useful. What a long and costly way to give us useful things, along with many disastrous ones, such as the chemicals which are destroying our soil, our waters, our very lives and those of countless of earth's creatures.

In a vastly more positive approach in the world of technology, there were those working to fulfill the commitment of President Kennedy, and on July 20, 1969, Neil Armstrong set foot upon the moon. What a celebration for the world! As we gathered around our television sets, we saw Neil Armstrong and Buzz Aldrin move across this desolate surface 238,857 miles from the Earth. We heard Armstrong's words, "That's one small step for man, one giant leap for mankind." We were overwhelmed and full of joy that human beings working together for a common objective could achieve so much.

I had the privilege of meeting Edgar Mitchell, the sixth man to walk upon the moon. He found it difficult to describe his feelings when he saw the Earth surrounded by darkness, but glowing with beauty. He knew then that we are all one and a part of a great and magnificent system. He told himself he would resign from the Navy and devote his life to the teaching of this fact. He was later to establish the Institute for Noetic Sciences in Palo Alto, a constantly growing organization.

The volunteer program at UCLA continued to develop. I had often thought of how wonderful it would be if individuals from countries across the world could come to appreciate the power each of us has to improve life not only for ourselves, but for all of life. Perhaps there could be worldwide volunteer programs. This was only a dream, until one day a lovely lady came into my office. Her name was Ruth Frankel from Toronto, Canada. She told me she had planned an international volunteer program for volunteers working in cancer institutes and she invited me to attend the initial meeting in the fall of 1968, along with my assistant, Virginia Clemens. We not only attended but met for six days with twenty-six volunteer leaders from eleven countries. We listened, we shared, we worked side by side with volunteers in hospitals and were inspired each moment relative to the power of the individual to make a difference in the lives of others. The experience of love and sharing was so profound that I knew it must go on to become an international program involving volunteers in every phase of life.

I returned to Los Angeles determined to make this a reality. This I did, for early in 1969 I invited a number of volunteer leaders in the L.A. community to meet at my home to discuss the possibility of forming an international association for volunteer education. It was an afternoon meeting and I remember serving champagne, hoping to have everyone in a receptive mood for such an undertaking. I found this was not necessary, for the idea was greeted with high enthusiasm. We all went to work immediately. George was asked to draw up the by-laws, which he did, as he was totally supportive. We received permission through Ruth Powlinson to use the magnificent mural from Occidental College. This mural depicted people from across the world gathering around the globe and we chose it as our symbol. It was beautiful, and was used for many years until it became too expensive to reproduce.

Many meetings followed during which time I relinquished my leadership role, for I believed firmly that a volunteer should lead a volunteer organization such as ours and at that time I was a paid employee of the University of California. I met with Mary Ripley, who was one of the most dynamic leaders in the city, and asked her if she would be willing to lead this organization. She agreed and became the first president and has ever since done a remarkable job in fulfilling our mission. I continued to work very diligently in the background. I wrote all of the invitational letters to prospective candidates for our first International Conference, securing names from the State Department and funds for those who could not attend without them, as well as raising funds for the conference itself. We sent 110 invitational letters with 59 responding and attending. They were from Afghanistan, Australia, the Bahamas, Brazil, Canada, Colombia, Costa Rica, Egypt, England,

Ethiopia, France, Germany, Honduras, Israel, Iran, Jamaica, Japan, Laos, Nicaragua, Nigeria, Pakistan, Panama, the Philippines, Switzerland, Thailand, USSR, Vietnam, and, of course, the United States. Since that time, International Conferences have taken place in the Philippines, Switzerland, Australia, England, Israel, Colombia, Buenos Aires, Japan, Singapore, San Francisco, France, Turkey, Canada, Amsterdam and Korea. The whole purpose of the International Conference was to bring people together from all over the world, unified by a common purpose of service to the needs of others, thereby helping to build bridges of understanding among people throughout the world.

One of the most exciting conferences was the one in Japan in 1982. Their planning was superb. We not only learned from one another, but experienced the beauties of their country. Japan to me is like another home. I have been there three times and each time I have wept when I left. The beauty and serenity of their gardens, together with the gentleness and hospitality of the people, have been magnificent gifts to me. The fact that our Joan's roommate at the University of Utah was a Japanese girl, studying to receive her graduate degree in social work, brought me ever closer to the Japanese people. She is like my third daughter. Her name is Takako Hashimoto Sankawa, now the mother of two grown girls and married to Dr. Hiroshi Sankawa, who was Medical Chief of the Tokyo Children's Hospital. I visited them when I attended the Regional International

Volunteer Conference in 1987 in Nagoya honoring my friend, Lois Howard, and me for helping to launch volunteer programs in Japan.

My dear friend, Lois Howard, a beautiful blonde with sparkling blue eyes, had lived in Japan for four years after the war with her West Point flyer husband. She not only learned the Japanese language, but graduated from several flower arranging schools there and proceeded to teach flower arranging to the Japanese on Japanese television in the Japanese language. Shortly after Lois, her husband and two children returned to the U.S., Lois' husband was killed in a plane crash. In making a new life for herself, she returned to school at UCLA and came to volunteer at the Medical Center. In those days we had many doctors visiting the center from Japan, so it was quite natural to assign Lois as their hostess and guide, an assignment given to volunteers with special skills in absorbing and imparting knowledge about the Medical Center and its many research, care and treatment facilities. The Japanese visitors were especially interested in learning about the volunteers who wore those aqua pinafores (slacks and jackets are the uniforms today). Lois was a good teacher for among other things, she imparted the information about the volunteers and their abilities to bring a dimension of warmth and caring, often relieving staff members, enabling them to extend their own skills. Without being aware of it, Lois planted seeds which grew well.

Chapter Eleven

*The highest reward for one's toil is not what
one gets for it, but what one becomes by it.*

—Henry Ward Beecher

Let me go back a few years prior to 1970, when George and I were enjoying many of our happiest years. As I mentioned earlier, we bought our home in 1962 in Santa Monica Canyon overlooking a beautiful garden and the Pacific Ocean, where we entertained our friends, enjoyed our nightly martinis, worked, read, and loved. One of our most rewarding experiences was a trip overseas with the first Stanford Alumni College. We were with a marvelous group of people, including Paul and Anne Ehrlich, well known for their work on the dire effects of population growth on this planet, Don Kennedy, later to become President of Stanford University, and the heads of the Political Science and Art departments. Our travels took us to Amsterdam, up the Rhine River to Basil, stopping at key cities and points of historical interest and beauty in Germany, then to Burgenstock above Lake Lucerne, on to Florence and ultimately to Paris, a magnificent experience for both of us. I especially remember Burgenstock. There were only three hotels and a few elegant shops, high in the mountains overlooking the lake. Before we left home I had taken several hundred dollars out of my savings account for the express purpose of buying myself a gold wrist watch. But upon arrival, I was so fascinated by the gorgeous linen shops and the elegant Swiss linens and embroideries that I spent all of my money on linen gifts for my friends. As a result, I came home without my gold watch. I must tell you, however, that I soon had one. It was exactly like the one I had visualized buying. It came as a result of a give-a-way for the lucky ticket I had purchased for a KCET benefit. Once again, we cannot give anything away without it returning in some form—not exactly the same, however, as was my gold watch.

During those early years in Santa Monica we had the pleasure of enjoying our grown daughters, their children, and our grandchildren. Dianne's firstborn was a boy, named Steven, followed by three daughters: Suzanne, Carolynne, and Jody. Joan and her husband, Max, have four sons: Jason, Matthew, Mark, and Ben. All together they have produced nine little ones, making me that many times a great-grandmother. They are all wonderful and I love them very much even though I am not one to carry pictures or baby-sit.

In 1975 I retired from my position at UCLA. I was overwhelmed by the events which took place, including a huge surprise luncheon at the famed Bistro restaurant in Beverly Hills. Over a hundred friends sang, read poems, laughed and enjoyed one another. My dear friend from 20th Century Fox days, Celeste Holm, flew out from New York to be the M.C. She played and sang many songs including the one which made her famous from the musical "Oklahoma" called "I Can't Say No" substituting "She" for "I."

On the same day when I arrived home I found a letter from Otis Chandler, the President of the Los Angeles Times, saying I had been selected for one of the 1975 Women of Achievement Awards. What an event this was! It took place at the auditorium of the paper with the city's notables offering their congratulations. Two other parties at the university, one by the Auxiliary and the other by the Medical Center staff, all took me into the clouds for weeks, and into a state of disbelief. The following weeks were spent writing thank you notes, as well as reflecting upon those wonderful and remarkable years at UCLA—none of which could have happened without the loyal support of my wonderful husband, George, who was always able and willing to listen with total love, compassion and understanding, giving encouragement all along the way.

Now I was a volunteer again! The first thing to happen was an invitation to join the Women's Council for KCET, the public TV station in Los Angeles. I was even asked if I would consider becoming president of this group, which I declined, not wishing any more leadership roles at this time. I enjoyed the council and especially working with the one-hundred talented and concerned women and friends I had known throughout the years.

One day in 1977 two of my great friends, Kay Croissant and Cathy Dees, both former teachers and writers, came for luncheon for the express purpose of discussing a plan for writing a book on reincarnation. Out of the blue, I said, "Instead of writing another book on reincarnation why don't we consider designing an exhibit on the fact that life is a continuum." I had the courage to do this because my friends, Norma Bowles and Fran Hynds, had opened an exhibit at the California Museum of Science and Industry called Psi Search, a rather far-out subject for this museum, so why not one on the immortality principle? I ran to the phone and called my friend, Bill McCann, the Director of the Museum, who astonished me by saying, "I have been waiting for someone to design an exhibit on this subject for years." An appointment was set up and soon an agreement was made that we would be given a 4000 square-foot room for the exhibit, which was scheduled to open in the spring of 1978. Within a few days after this meeting, Kay and Cathy went to work on the research and design while I set out to raise the funds. The exhibit opened as scheduled and was magnificent. Our exhibit room had very high ceilings, which added to the spaciousness. We painted the whole room black, so nothing was seen but the exhibits themselves, which were well lit. The panels were 90" high and 40" wide, with a number of free standing forms such as several laboratory bottles filled with the components of the human body: 65% water, 15% protein, 10% fats, 9% minerals, 1% carbohydrates. Statements were made by great teachers and philosophers such as Emerson who said, "When we speak with a person, we are looking at the individual exterior, but the actual 'person' to whom we are speaking remains invisible to us."

Another freestanding exhibit was a hologram of a young woman in pain, a suicide, with statements by Plato and others relative to suicides. Set into one of the walls was a television screen with Elisabeth Kubler-Ross speaking on death and dying. Through the beautiful paintings of great philosophers and teachers from ancient Egypt to Einstein, there was little doubt expressed as to the fact that life is a continuum. As I said before, Thomas Edison was endeavoring to develop a machine or apparatus which could record persons who had died and moved to a higher plane. He gave interviews on this subject to Scientific American and American magazines in 1920. Unfortunately, he died prior to its completion.

The theses for the exhibit were that matter is not limited to the perceptions of the five senses; that energy is indestructible, that consciousness can exist independent of the physical body; that there is no proof that consciousness ends at death and much evidence that it continues.

Over a million individuals saw the exhibit and many letters came to us telling us that it changed their lives. That museum meant much to me even before the exhibit was presented there, for when I was at UCLA I was honored to be given the Merit Award by the Committee of Advanced Scientific Training at the University of Southern California for my work with students in helping them find their way into scientific careers. I did not do this alone, for members of my staff, especially Evie Conteas, our student volunteer coordinator, did much to inspire young people to follow scientific careers.

Chapter Twelve

The sheer folly of trying to defend a nation by
destroying all life on this planet must be apparent
to anyone capable of rational thought. Nuclear
capability must be reduced to zero, globally,
permanently. There is no other option.

—*Queen Noor of Jordan*

In 1978 I was asked to become the third president of the International Association for Volunteer Education (now Volunteer Effort). The Bicentennial Conference was to be held in Istanbul, Turkey. A plan was developed to combine the journey there with American Women for International Understanding, as most of us belonged to the two organizations. Ten of us made the journey, which began in Washington, D.C. at a dinner given by the ambassador from Jordan. We planned to go to Jordan, Egypt and Tunisia prior to landing in Turkey, meeting women of like mind wherever we went.

In Jordan we had not arranged to meet with anyone, for our plan was to go only to Petra to see those marvelous ruins. This was not to be, however, for as the plane landed, a voice came over the loudspeaker asking

Dr. Cory to please meet the captain upon deplaning. Dr. Genevieve Cory was one of our group. We were all amazed and could not imagine why she was singled out. Apparently, having the title of doctor made her seem more impressive. By the time she met with the captain, we had all deplaned. We were then taken to the king's waiting room where we were served tea. Obviously we were royal guests, but why? Oh yes, the Jordanian ambassador must have sent the word. We were not protesting, but how were we to get to Petra!? After tea we were escorted into three Mercedes cars and driven to our hotel with word that we were to meet them in the lobby at 8:00 the next morning. This we did and began a day always to be remembered. First we drove to the University of Jordan where we met the Dean of the Political Science Department who gave us a brief history of Jordan. Returning to the cars, we took off again, driving 100 miles per hour on narrow dirt roads. I knew we would never return alive and finally I said, "Eleanor, you are going to have to die sometime, so why not now?"

Our next stop was a village on the West Bank where we saw the simplicity in which people were living in an attempt to make a statement to the world as to the need to reclaim their territories. Three of the Palestinian leaders met with the ten of us. Looking at these three bearded gentlemen in their turbans and long robes, we felt like lambs to the slaughter. Instead, they pleaded with us to speak to our government leaders in their behalf. We smiled and said very little. Surely, if greater endeavors had been made then to restore a homeland for the Palestinians, the acts of terrorism would not exist as they do today.

Back to the cars for another mad journey to Jeresch, the most well-known Roman ruins. Having seen many, I understand its reputation. There is a long street lined with tall and magnificent Roman columns leading to the coliseum. We felt the drama as we visualized the pageantry which took place there so many centuries ago. We lingered in this ancient city, where we were served a delightful luncheon under the trees as our minds traveled back in time.

Our next stop was at a youth center, seeing the athletic facilities for hundreds of young people, then on to meet Princess Basma, the sister of King Hussein. She, like her brother, devoted her life to better education and living conditions for her people She wanted to hear from each of us as to our own activities in America. She was a warm and beautiful woman and we were extremely grateful for the opportunity to meet with her.

Then we went for tea at the home of a former ambassador to the U.S., where we met with presidents of various businesses and corporations. We were the only women among a room full of men. It was so arranged that each of us had a conversation with the men present, learning from one another. Finally we were returned to our hotel to collapse with gratitude to the drivers who go 100 miles per hour—without them we couldn't have seen and learned so much. But collapse we did not do, for we were told that a formal dinner was being given for us. It was there we met Zena Rodenko who, at that time, was one of the educational leaders of Jordan. It was instant friendship and since that splendid dinner she has visited us in the U.S. and we still have a warm relationship by phone and letter.

The following morning we were picked up by Zena and taken to a number of museums prior to boarding a plane for Cairo, Egypt. Petra would wait for another time.

Egypt was as wonderful as our dreams. In addition to seeing its beauties, we met many of the women leaders and visited various agencies, the Leper Institute, schools, hospitals and the inner workings of the city. Such opportunities are not provided for the average tourist. We then spent several days in Tunisia, a lovely land, both modern and ancient. Their leader had very democratic concepts as to how he should govern, so we felt a sense of freedom in this lovely land overlooking the Mediterranean Sea.

Finally we landed at the airport in Istanbul, to see many huge banners saying "Welcome to IAVE!" What a good feeling this was in such a faraway place. Perihan Ariburan was the chair. She was a poet, and the wife of the former General of the Turkish Army. She met us with loving arms. We were driven to the Istanbul Hilton, which at that time was the finest hotel there overlooking the Bosphorus. I was rooming with Lois Howard. We could not have been happier as we stood on our balcony across the waters dividing Turkey from the Soviet Union. That evening there was a very formal dinner at a private club. There were about fifty of us with the Turkish members and those coming from other nations. We were seated at one long table on only one side, so we all had a view of the Bosphorus with a full golden moon rising out of the waters. The rest of our stay in Istanbul continued to be full of beauty and drama in addition to our educational programs. I felt very privileged to be the leader of this group sharing the various ways we could volunteer for the good of all people and all nations. At our last meeting there, General Ariburan arose and said, "Men have been ruling the world for centuries and we still do not have peace. From what I have seen and heard during this past week, I believe the women of the world can do it." We felt proud and challenged and still carry his words in our hearts with the hope that someday his vision will become a reality.

It is now many years later and still terrorism prevails. Have we not worked enough for peace, for justice and the rights and recognition of all people? Unfortunately we have not. Thousands of children die of starvation each day and over 200 million people have died in wars during the 20th Century. When will we be able to make the lives of others as important as our own? I believe that then, and only then, will we be able to eliminate acts of terrorism in our world.

Chapter Thirteen

Spontaneous relationship to man and nature
connects the individual with the world without
eliminating his or her individuality.

—Erich Fromm

Toward the end of the 1970s I became aware of a change in my George's behavior. He had moments of becoming irrational, unlike his gentle self. He was also very forgetful. I knew something was wrong, so I took him to a number of doctors, including my longtime friend, Augustus Rose, the Head of the Department of Neurology at UCLA. He merely said, "George is growing old and a bit senile." I knew within myself that it was more than that. In addition to his not remembering and being incoherent, there were moments when he became hostile, which was totally contrary to his nature. No one diagnosed his problem as being Alzheimer's disease, but finally doctors seemed to surmise that it was more than senility; therefore, it must be Alzheimer's.

While George was still living, I had the good fortune of having a marvelous friend living in the next block who loved George and would come to stay with him for several hours at a time, giving me relief and the opportunity to continue working in the community. At that time my chief work was against the building of nuclear arms. A small group met every week in the offices of Claire Townsend, who was Vice President of 20th Century-Fox. My dear friend, Suzy Marks, introduced me to this group, where I met two of my closest friends, Pauline and Richard Saxon, as well as others such as Ross Merrin, who is now Vice President of Distribution for Sony Films. We formed an organization called Communicators for Social Responsibility. The majority of the members were involved in the media and we all wanted to send a message to the world regarding the need to abandon the building of nuclear weapons. We presented a number of remarkable programs with speakers such as Helen Caldicott and Norman Cousins. It seems that nothing has changed, for we continue to spend billions on arms. We do not know, however, what effect we had on raising consciousness, but I do believe every action does have an effect upon the whole. The learning process is slow and we must continue to act, to give the best we can to make a better world and never lose hope.

During this period I was also working with Lois Howard on a fund-raiser for a new Japanese pavilion at the Los Angeles County Museum of Art. Among other things, we sold raffle tickets for $10 each for a drawing that provided a trip to China for two. I bought three, tucked them away in my wallet, and forgot about them.

The event took place on March 28, 1981. What a magnificent event it was! Lois never does anything halfway or without rare beauty and creativity. It was a formal ball held in one of the 1923 classical buildings of that era. There were large, beautiful, high ceilings and wide stairways leading to the ballroom. After enjoying a superb Chinese dinner, Keye Luke, a well-known actor and a friend of mine, came to the stage and drew the winning number for the trip to China. Yes, you have guessed, it was one of my numbers, a Lindblad tour to China and Japan for two!

At that time George was not with me, for the effects of Alzheimer's disease caused him to become hostile and totally disoriented in crowds or outside of his own environment. On my way home from the ball I could hardly wait to tell George what had happened, for we had always dreamed of going to China together. I am sure we lived there happily with one another in former lives, for we always felt a close affinity to this country.

That night I lost my own sense of reality. As I returned home, I rushed to the side of the bed and awakened George to tell him we could now go to China. Reality returned all too quickly, however, when George failed to respond and deep sadness replaced my joyful heart.

The next morning I began thinking about the trip and the possibilities of taking someone with me. Who would it be? Surely one of my daughters, but how could I choose which one? After much contemplation, I decided to invite a person I also loved and in whose company I enjoyed some of my happiest hours, Ann Chamberlain. Of course, she was delighted and I have always been grateful that we had this magical time together. Ann's humor, her great appreciation for all that is beautiful and her joy in living were very special gifts to me. I still hope my Dianne and Joan will be able to take part of their inheritance and visit these wonderful lands someday.

We had much advice as to what to take to China at that time, which included more disinfectants than on the shelves of most drugstores. Fortunately, we unloaded them as we traveled from city to city. Except for one day when Ann was ill with a cold, we remained healthy.

Ann and I departed on a beautiful fall day in 1981. My darling daughter, Dianne, came to stay with her father while we would be away. We were totally prepared for the long flight to the extent that I had even made a hand-painted cardboard set of rummy tiles, a game with tiles similar to Mah Jong tiles, played much like gin rummy, but a bit more challenging. Ann and I had an addiction to this game, so we knew we could play it all the way to China. The tiles were laid out in the open space between us as we flew toward Alaska, going north before crossing the ocean to the magical lands of the East. Rather than continuing our flight, however, the plane landed in Anchorage, Alaska. We were asked to deplane and walk about a bit as there was a technical problem which would soon be resolved. The latter proved not to be true, however, and after about an hour we boarded another plane with the assurance that all of our personal belongings had been transferred, all but the rummy tiles! Apparently we were not to play games, but to think of the excitement of the days ahead. After a 16-hour flight, we were happy to see the lights of Hong Kong reflected in the waters surrounding the airport. We were met by a lovely young woman from Lindblad Tours who was to be our leader for the next two weeks. Ann and I were taken to our hotel and were ecstatic when we saw the luxury of our room, which was very large and beautifully furnished, with a refrigerator holding anything we might have desired and a magnificent view of the bay. There was no time for indulging, however, only time for a quick shower before we were expected downstairs to meet the other fifteen members of the tour who came from various cities throughout the United States and Canada. I cannot really remember much about any of those people except the two who sat across the table from us. Our eyes met as if we had always known one another. They were a young couple, obviously in love, by the names of Shep Secter, a dentist, and Marina Paperney, a lawyer. She is now a judge and they are the devoted parents of two children, ages eleven and fifteen. We chatted during dinner, learning more about one another. This was just the beginning of two remarkable weeks of friendship and sharing all along the way. Once again, how can such close relationships happen instantaneously unless we had been friends before in another life? Although my wonderful friend, Ann, died in 1993, Shep and Marina and I keep in touch. Their pictures are on my dresser with Ann's and those of other friends and relatives whom I love.

Traveling in China in 1981 was quite different from today. There were no new hotels, as I understand there are now, and comparatively few travelers. We had the privilege of staying in Angler's Lodge in Peking (now Beijing) which at present is off limits to everyone except foreign diplomats. It consists of beautiful summer guest houses which were built by the Empress of China during the nineteenth century. They are in the midst of beautiful gardens with bridges over winding streams and lakes. Each guest house has a number of magnificent bedrooms with extremely high ceilings, wide stairways and lovely scrolls and tapestries throughout the huge lobby and other rooms. It is several miles from the heart of the city. The gates are locked and no one enters or leaves without an official, which in our case was our guide.

One night toward the end of our visit to Peking, we all boarded a bus to go to the city for a very special Peking duck dinner and to see the center of Peking on a Saturday night. The bus driver said he would let us out on the corner of the main street, but would pick us up after our dinner at the restaurant, which was several blocks away. The streets were teeming with people all looking alike to us, dressed the same in black pants and white coolie jackets. Generally, Ann and I were among the first to descend from the bus, but this night we were busy talking and were the last ones off. The others had moved ahead out of sight. It apparently was not until the others reached the restaurant that they realized we were not following them. At first Ann and I were not disturbed, for we thought we could find a restaurant specializing in Peking duck. If not, we would ask. As it happened, there were such restaurants on every corner. No one, but no one, spoke English. We went in and out of shops, stopped people on the street and were greeted with vacant looks and no responses. Here we were in the center of Peking, surrounded by what seemed like, and probably were, millions of Chinese people speaking no English. Even if they had, we didn't know where we were going. There were no taxis, only bicycles. We walked like crazed people, not having the faintest notion of what to do or where to go. Finally, we saw a camera shop advertising Eastman Kodak. All of a sudden we felt we had found a touch of America. Surely we would find help there, but no. Even if we had found help, what would we say? With no taxis, how would we get back to Angler's Lodge and even if we had, we wouldn't be able to get in without our guide. Maybe we could go to a hotel and spend the night, but where was a hotel? Just at that moment, we saw a Caucasian man entering one of the shops. We latched onto him as we would a life preserver in deep waters. He was from Canada and very kind. He pointed out the direction of the nearest and biggest hotel in Peking, many blocks away. We literally ran to what we knew would be our safety zone and so it was. Our tour leader was already there and we fell into her arms. She was wise enough to assume we would do what we did. We were taken back to the restaurant, but by then it was time to return to the lodge. Our friends were worried and we were distressed that by not keeping our eyes open, we had not exactly enhanced our "evening on the town."

With the exception of that one night, visiting Peking was a remarkable experience. We were in awe of the Great Wall of China, the tombs, Tiananmen Square, wide streets and the millions of bicycles (replaced today by motor cars). Wandering through the Forbidden Palace, feasting on the beauties of the Summer Palace of the Empress with its lakes and gardens took us back to another place, another time.

From Peking, we went on to Shanghai. We stayed in what was once an exclusive club for the British. It must have been built in the early 1920s with its huge built-in wardrobes made of the finest bleached mahogany for the extensive wardrobes of the rich. While it was very beautiful, it left us with a feeling of decadence, of a misused woman of beauty, long discarded. I could not help thinking of the wielding power ending in a bloody revolution years later, never to be completely resolved. Once again, there can never be a positive result from negative actions, be it an individual or a nation.

The best of all our experiences in China was being

in Guilin. As we stepped from the bus, we found ourselves in a magical valley with a silver thread running through it which was the river Li. As we stood on its shores, we were totally speechless by the beauties before us. We knew now why so many works of art depict mountains ascending into the air like huge petals of flowers rising from the earth. It would be impossible to describe such beauty. During the three days we were there we explored the caves under the mountains, climbed hundreds of stairs to observe the magnificent views, traveled on the river, saw the many fishermen on their bamboo rafts with their cormorants tied to their rafts with rings around their necks as a type of leash. The birds would spot a fish, dive into the water to retrieve it and then the fisherman would pull on the leash, extracting the fish from the mouth of the bird. We hoped the birds were rewarded for their work by the end of the day.

While we were in Guilin we observed Ann's birthday at a dinner in our small hotel for the whole group. The highlight of the evening was a typical Communist cake, Bright Red with yellow Chinese lettering, which we were told said "Happy Birthday." In any culture, friendship and good wishes are always cherished, as they were that night of September 22, 1981.

We were deeply impressed not only in Guilin, but in all the cities we visited, by parents, men and women, caring for a single child with unbelievable pride. This they knew was to be their only child. Having more than one child placed a heavy toll upon the family income, which they knew would be heavily reduced by Communist law. China was the highest populated country in the world, and there are already too many mouths to feed.

As we left China, we were full of high expectations, for we were on our way to Japan. Ann and I knew we had lived in both China and Japan in other lives, but we were not sure which one would bring back the happiest memories. As we walked into our hotel room in Tokyo, finding it full of flowers, kimonos laid out for us on the beds, we laughed and said, "This is it." The feeling of being home, which we continued to feel in Japan, was a beautiful gift for both of us.

Soon we would be joining my Japanese daughter and her family. I have told you about her before, but now I shall tell you exactly how she became my daughter. The first year our daughter, Joan, was at the University of Utah, she was asked by the Dean of Students if she would be willing to get an apartment and live with a Japanese girl who was so homesick that she was fearful for her life. She felt comfortable asking Joan, for the Dean and I had gone to kindergarten together. She was also aware that Joan was a warm, understanding and giving person. Of course Joan said "yes." From that time on, Joan's new roommate, Takako Hashimoto, whom we call Becca, became her sister and ultimately our daughter. While she had a loving family in Tokyo, we were her second family, an arrangement that continues to this day.

Becca not only stayed with us whenever she was in Los Angeles, but George had the privilege of giving her away when she was married to Hiroshi Sankawa, a Japanese doctor who was at the L.A. Children's Hospital doing his residency. At the time of their marriage, her mother was ill and could not attend the wedding. Shortly thereafter, however, her mother and father flew all the way from Japan to thank us personally for Becca's wedding which, I must say, was a beautiful occasion. Our house, with its huge deck overlooking the ocean, was made for such a summer wedding. Added to the beauties of the surroundings was Becca herself in a magnificent Japanese wedding kimono of gold and white brocade, plus other Japanese women guests in their lovely kimonos. How sad that this tradition is no longer popular!

Going to Tokyo to see Becca and Sandy (Hiroshi) and their two daughters I knew would be a wonderful experience. And so it was, from the moment we saw Becca standing at the airport to greet us until the sad moment when we departed. Of course, seeing "my children" again was the best gift, as well as meeting their children, Kasumi and Misa, then teenagers. Flowers, gifts, journeys to the magnificent countryside, lunches, dinners presented as works of art, visits to the shrines and temples all added to our many marvelous experiences and memories bringing us back to a land we knew and loved. Tears welled in our eyes as we departed. It was like leaving our home and part of our family.

Chapter Fourteen

If we are serious about stopping terrorism,
then our goal must be to reduce the level of
fear, injustice and poverty in the world.

—*John Robbins*

When I returned home, I continued my work with Physicians for Social Responsibility in the endeavor to stop the building of nuclear arms. One of our endeavors was getting signatures for what was called Proposition 12, which would have banned the further building of these deadly weapons. I held signs on street corners and on Wilshire Boulevard in lines going into theaters on Saturday nights, and all those things activists do. When the vote came up on Proposition 12, we won with 85% of the voters giving support. Similar propositions were passed across the country. Unfortunately, the arms manufacturers were too powerful, as they still are today and nothing has changed. We continue spending billions of dollars to build arms while one out of four children go to bed hungry each night in this, the wealthiest nation in the world. Is it going to take an economic collapse or another major catastrophe to awaken the hearts and minds of those who seem to make money their God?

George's illness continued to occupy most of my waking hours. Fortunately, he usually slept until noon, so I could accomplish a good deal prior to his awakening. After that, however, we were busy, for George wanted to go to the office which, of course, had been closed. We usually drove there, stopped in front, and then George was ready to leave and return home. This same procedure often happened in the middle of the night when he insisted he had an appointment. He would get up and dress then insist that I do the same and became very hostile until I did. For such a gentle man, it was difficult seeing this type of behavior. It finally became so difficult that in the fall of 1984 I decided to take George to the Motion Picture Home in the San Fernando Valley. My dear friend, Bill Tiller, a Stanford professor, author of "Science and Human Transformation," and very spiritual person, knew I had always said that I would never put anyone I loved in a nursing home. As a result, he suggested that I sit down on the side of George's bed while he was sleeping and speak to him mentally, telling him of my plans. This I did. The next morning I sat by him on his bed and said, "Darling, because of your illness you are sometimes hostile, which makes me afraid. For this reason, I am going to take you to the Motion Picture Home. I will come to see you every day and will love you always." As I finished, George spoke to me and said,

"Dearest, continue doing your work, do not be afraid and be safe." I was overcome with the knowledge that his higher mind was still intact. I cried with joy in this knowledge for I knew I would see him again as he had always been, a wonderful, kind and intelligent man. He went on sleeping and when he awakened he was just as "out of it" as he had been.

Prior to taking George to the Motion Picture Home, I met with a social worker to make plans for a comfortable transition. It was agreed that I would share a room with him for several nights until he felt comfortable being in a new environment. It didn't work out that way, for the staff felt it would be better if he were in a room across from the nursing station so they could better care for him. Unfortunately, I acquiesced. Both Joan and Dianne were with me that sad day as we left my wonderful husband and lover of so many years. It became even sadder as the days unfolded and I learned that the entire staff at the time, including the doctors, knew nothing about caring for an Alzheimer's patient. Instead of being gentle and changing the subject if he became troublesome, they fought him. The day Dianne, Joan and I took him to the Home, he was able to bathe and dress himself. He always insisted upon wearing a suit, vest, and tie even through the summer days. He was as meticulous as he was handsome. That was the last day he ever dressed himself. In fact, he became totally dependent. When I saw this overnight change, I wept bitter tears for what I had allowed to happen. My only consolation was in knowing his higher consciousness was still there, as was proven to me a few days earlier.

Four months after George entered the Motion Picture Home, he died of kidney failure, fortunately without pain. He just went to sleep. Prior to his death he had lost his capacity to communicate, but as I left him the night before he died, I hugged him and expressed my love. He in turn slurred words saying "I.. I.. I.. love you." This we had said and felt every day of our lives together. While Dianne and I went home that night, Joan sat with her father throughout the night until he left his body, a great sadness and a blessing. Two weeks later we had a memorial for George, inviting his closest friends to the house for champagne and reminiscing about the fun, the wisdom and the joys George had brought into the lives of each of us.

I continued to work closely with my good friend, Dorothy Kirsten French, in founding the French Foundation for Alzheimer's Research. Dorothy's husband, Dr. John French, a neurologist and Director of the UCLA Brain Research Institute, also had Alzheimer's disease. Dorothy was determined to do something about this dreaded disease. She said, "I am going to raise money, but not so a doctor can sit in a laboratory and ultimately win a Nobel Prize. I am going to raise enough money to bring doctors together from across the world to share their knowledge until an answer is found." For many years Dorothy was one of the most revered opera stars at the Metropolitan Opera Company, as well as a star in motion pictures. She was beautiful and dynamic. When she set her heart and mind to a project, it became a reality.

George and Jack were both still alive when we set out to form an organization and raise funds. One of the highlights of this venture was meeting Richard Eamer, then President of the National Medical Enterprises. A date was made to meet him in his office. At that time he was listed in the Forbes Report as one of the nine wealthiest men in the U.S.A. As we sat waiting for him in his inner office I said to Dorothy, "Don't be so nervous, this is a very kind man. Don't you see, he has pictures of horses and dogs all over his walls?" I knew that anyone loving animals had to be kind and gentle. When he walked in it was like a fresh breeze. He was a man in his fifties wearing a sports jacket and open shirt and he had a very relaxed demeanor. He sat down, put his hands on his knees and said, "Now what do you want of me? Money, to sit on your board of directors or build a hospital for you?" Dorothy, always being quick to reply, said, "All three!" Thus the French Foundation for Alzheimer's Research was launched. Dick, as he became lovingly known to Dorothy and me, did respond with all three. The first hospital for Alzheimer's disease opened in November of 1987 in a small community near Long Beach, California. The Foundation budget is now in the millions. Dorothy died in 1992, but her dream did come true for doctors from across the world meet in Los Angeles each year to share their knowledge.

Along with my other interests during the decade of the 1980s, was my ongoing work with friends against the continued building of nuclear arms. This brought me into the offices of Physicians for Social Responsibility with my dear friends, Richard Saxon, President of PSR and his beloved wife, Pauline, who gave up her own career as a child therapist to spend every day in the office. Two of my most exciting adventures during this period were trips to the Soviet Union with Pauline and Richard and other members of PSR. I shall never forget that first journey, as we flew over what was then Leningrad, seeing the many tall, drab, gray buildings, the homes of the majority of Soviet citizens. As we landed and approached the city, however, we found it to be magnificent. It was one of the first cities in the world to be built according to a professional plan. While the master plan was under the direction of a Russian architect, others came from France, Italy, Switzerland, and Germany. We felt privileged as we checked into our hotel on the Nevi River, where we had spectacular views of the many bridges and beautiful buildings, including L'Hermitage. Never mind the cockroaches in our room!

Marjorie Braude, a psychiatrist from Los Angeles, was my roommate. She ran back and forth across those bridges every morning, apparently a rare sight for the citizens, but health-giving to Marjorie. Both of us felt the vigor of the White Nights, for we were there in June when it is daylight for 19 hours out of every 24. Our tours of the city and its environs, including the Summer Palace, were marvelous. The best gift of all, of course, was meeting the Soviet people, who were quite wonderful and were longing for a world without fears, just as we were. In addition to the doctors we met whose interests coincided with those of PSR, we spent one morning with members of the Soviet Women's Committee. When Pauline suggested to them that we form an ongoing dialogue with them, the chairperson said, "Do you not know that such a dialogue was begun in 1968 with a group from American Women for International Understanding?" She went on to name some of them. I exclaimed, "These are all friends of mine and I am also a member of this organization." Once again I realized how close we are to one another as a part of this vast universe.

After leaving Leningrad, now St. Petersburg, we flew to Moscow, our destination for the conference we would be attending by the International Physicians for the Prevention of Nuclear War. This organization was founded by Dr. Bernard Lown of Harvard and Dr. Eugene Chazov from the Soviet Union. These two compassionate and learned men realized we must be able to speak to one another if we are to have peace in the world. Once again I am reminded of the power of individuals. Such actions as theirs opened the door to the end of the cold war.

Moscow, the center of scientific, economic, and

political life, this is truly a dramatic city. Red Square was even larger than we had imagined it to be. In addition to touring the city, going to the ballet and seeing their legendary circus, most of our time was spent at the huge Conference Center listening and participating in workshops and meeting people of like mind from around the world.

Our second trip to the Soviet Union was in 1987 to attend another such conference. Following the conference experience, a few of us stayed on to visit Kiev and Yalta for our own enlightenment and pleasure. I found Kiev to be another beautiful city, with lovely old trees lining all of the streets. This was the home of the renowned poet, Alexander Pushkin. We were constantly reminded of this man, who must have been much beloved, for statues of him were everywhere.

During our flight from Moscow to Kiev and Yalta, my seat mate was a lady named Bronia Hatfield, a psychiatrist from Australia. As we spoke, we learned that we both shared a common philosophy believing in reincarnation to the extent that we knew we had been friends in another life. She shared her experiences in this one, which were unbelievable for a person like myself who has had so little misfortune.

We found Yalta to be another beautiful city, reminding me very much of Santa Barbara, with mountains in the background and the city on the shores of the Black Sea. We stayed in a huge, but very pleasant hotel which was built by the government as one of the many resort hotels for vacations for the Soviet workers, all expenses paid by the government.

The second day we were in Yalta, we went to the palace where the Peace Agreements were signed by Churchill, Stalin and Roosevelt after World War II. During our return in the bus to the hotel in the late afternoon Bronia said to me, "Eleanor, that Peace Agreement didn't mean a thing. Now we must sign another one." I couldn't understand what she was talking about, but she was persistent. She said, "Tomorrow we are going to meet with all the city officials and TV crews (at that time there were only three television stations in all of Russia), get into our skirts and get the men into their ties and coats, and go to the spot we just left and sign another Agreement." I said, "Bronia, you must be mad. It's four o'clock now. How do you propose to do this?" She said, "Eleanor, I was born Polish and Jewish, I was only fourteen years old when I saw the Nazis kill my mother and father and all my friends. Because I was able to hide I escaped, but for two years I continued to hide without having adequate food and shelter. I was eventually rescued by the Russian military." Bronia was up all night contacting the three TV stations and writing a new Peace Agreement as a symbol of our desire for peace. During the day she contacted the various city officials and by 4:00 p.m. there was a formal meeting in Yalta where once again a Peace Agreement was signed. This was covered by all the TV stations and the press with headlines in the papers with accompanying pictures. Bronia taught many of us that all things are possible where there is a will and a faith. This was but another example of one person following the dictates of her heart and having the power to do so because she believed it was possible. I believe so totally that there is a Universal power which responds to such faith.

We flew back to Moscow where Bronia and I parted as the close friends we had always been. Since then she has visited me several times and we speak with one another frequently.

Chapter Fifteen

Love is the only force capable of
transforming an enemy into a friend.
*   —Martin Luther King, Jr.*

On a hot summer day in 1992, I found myself in Jericho in one of the three offices of Yasser Arafat, meeting with his Chief of Staff, Dr. Sami Musallam, a warm, highly educated gentleman. The next day I was in Tunis, in another of Arafat's offices, speaking with his Minister of Education, Mr. Yasser Abed Rabbo, a person of similar high qualities to those of Dr. Musallam's. In our conversations I learned that both men had survived long years of ordeals, in and out of prison. Their lives were single-pointedly devoted to finding peace with the Israelis and freedom for the Palestinian people. I could not help thinking that Yasser Arafat himself must be an intelligent man to have such executives as these at his side. I later learned that if I had been able to stay in Tunis another day I would have met him as well.

I say "I," but I was not alone. I was there in the

Middle East with a small group under the leadership of Scott Kennedy, Mayor of Santa Cruz, whose dedication to the cause of peace had taken him there many times before. The whole experience was made more pleasant and meaningful because my daughter, Joan, was part of the group. Her own professional work and background involve working with people of all races and religions, bringing great love and understanding all along the way.

Our meetings in Arafat's offices were just two of the privileged and extraordinary experiences we were to have on that visit to the Middle East. We stayed in a Palestinian Hotel in East Jerusalem across from the Garden Tomb believed by many to be the site of the burial and resurrection place of Jesus outside the walled city of Jerusalem. Our hotel was simple, the atmosphere and the people warm and friendly. We had our breakfasts and some of our dinners under a lovely grape arbor, which was conducive to great pleasure and relaxation.

Every morning we met with a person of prominence from Israel or Palestine, who spoke with us answering questions and sharing knowledge. I wish I could remember the names and titles of these marvelous and well informed people. I do remember, however, that they were political figures, artists and historians all desiring peace for their people. At the conclusion of these morning sessions, we were greeted by Zoughbi Zoughbi, Founder and Director of Wi'am, the Palestinian Conflict Resolution Center. Zoughbi became our friend, councilor and guide, taking us in and out of places the average tourist could not see. We were in East Jerusalem when we saw truckloads of young Israeli soldiers with their guns, running from home to home looking for Palestinians who might have crossed the borders "illegally." We sat with families who were weeping a few hours after their homes had been bombed for seemingly no reason. We spent one night in a West Bank hotel, saw the children playing in the gutters, and saw poverty everywhere.

One of the most interesting and inspiring days was spent with Dr. Hanna Nasir, the President of BirZeit University, and his wife. This is a few miles north of Ramallah which is almost fourteen miles north of Jerusalem. They had returned from Jordan only the day before, where they had been exiled by the Israelis for a number of years. He continued to serve the university, however, from afar. During our visit with Dr. Nasir and his lovely wife, I asked her if by any chance she knew my friend, Zena Rodenko in Jordan. She hastened to say, "Zena was my closest friend during the years we were there." Once again, are we all a part of one another? Do we have links with others around the world as well as those whom we see each day? I believe we do.

One day the women members of our group stood in the French Square in West Jerusalem (Israeli side) with other women from Israel and Palestine. All of us were in black as this was a weekly event called "Women in

Black", a vigil for peace. The responses from the general public were both positive and negative, the latter being more offensive.

On one of our last days in the Middle East we had a vision implanted in our hearts and in our minds which will last forever. We visited the Israeli Museum, Yad Vashem, in the Children's exhibit for the Holocaust. We walked into a dark and silent space with a narrow walkway, seeing nothing but stars all around us and soon heard the voices of different children. "I am Rebecca, I was ten," then another, "I am Joshua, I was six," then another, "I am Samuel, I was seven." This went on throughout our walk in the dark sky until we again reached daylight. There were no words to express our feelings, only tears.

The last day we were there we saw many young teenagers dancing, singing and laughing together in the streets of Jerusalem. Our greatest wish as we flew back to Rome, our place of departure, was that all the children of the Middle East and the world will one day be singing, dancing and laughing together.

Chapter Sixteen

With perseverance, well-directed application and the spirit of doing one's best, there can be no failure.

—George Wasson

In the fall of 1988 a group from PSR met in their offices to discuss what we should do about the environment, which was being threatened by destruction of forests and pollution of the lands, the air and the seas. One of the doctors, Dr. Samuel Roth, suggested we have a conference similar to the one held a few years before when the film, "Race to Oblivion," was shown and Dr. Helen Caldicott spoke with such fervor that the 3,000 people present shuddered at the possible destruction of the earth by selfishness and greed. We all concurred that not much had really changed since that day, so we must try again reminding ourselves that evolution moves slowly. Shortly after that first meeting, I left to attend a meeting in Washington, D.C. of the International Association for Volunteer Effort. While I was away, the committee members made me the chairperson for the planning of this conference. I wasn't there to protest, but obviously this was an honor and one I could not reject.

There were twenty of us on the committee. We met every week for seven months, securing the finest and best known environmentalists in the world. They included Martin Khor Kok Peng from Malaysia, Amory Lovins, Head of the Rocky Mountain Institute, Stephen Schneider, Head of the National Center for Atmospheric Research, David Suzuki, Professor of Biology, University of British Columbia, Prime Minister Gro Brundtland, physician and Prime Minister of Norway, and many others. In addition to the speakers, artists from throughout the Los Angeles area made magnificent collages of animals and the environment, which were placed over the columns and on the walls at the Bonaventure Hotel where the symposium was held. The first Resource Guide for Individual Action was designed and published for distribution at the Symposium and beyond. Physicians for Social Responsibility, Beyond War and the UCLA Medical Extension Division became the joint sponsors. Three thousand people were in attendance, including a chieftain from the Brazilian rain forests who pleaded with all those present to save his native lands.

During the planning for this symposium, I attended a weekend seminar at the Beyond War Conference Center 'midst the giant redwood forest just north of Santa Cruz. As I was driving back to Los Angeles I looked at those trees and told myself how marvelous it would be to live among them. I believe every thought produces a reaction and this one surely did.

An amazing change in my life occurred during the planning of the symposium, which I can only attribute to the angels. Perhaps you can find a better answer. As we were about to send copy to print for the symposium invitations, we received word from Robert Redford, who was to be our luncheon speaker, that he was asked to do a film and had to cancel. In fairness to him, we had been told that if this should happen he would have to accept. We called a meeting immediately at which time someone said, "Does anyone know John Robbins, the author of the acclaimed book, "Diet for a New America?" At that time no one knew John, so we called Noel Brown, Director for the Environment in the Northern Hemisphere for the United Nations. He told us he would accept providing he could change his plans. The next day after our meeting, a young friend from whom I had not heard in several years called me. I was delighted, saying, "Tony, where do you live and what are you doing?" Her answer amazed me for she said, "I live in Santa Cruz and I am working with John Robbins." This is only the beginning. Three days later another young friend called saying, "Eleanor, my apologies for calling you so late, but will you join me for breakfast tomorrow morning at the Beverly Hills Hotel to hear John Robbins?" I not only accepted, but was placed at his table with his wife and son. When I heard him speak, I knew he would make a fine replacement for Robert Redford. I asked if he would be free on May 13th, the day of the symposium. As it happened, he was, and Noel Brown was unable to change his plans, so John became our luncheon speaker and I had the privilege of introducing him,

From that day on, after I met John Robbins, for two weeks every single person I met spoke in some way about Santa Cruz. They were casual things like "My son is going to the University of California Santa Cruz" or "We are planning to go to Santa Cruz for the weekend." They were little comments but all involving Santa Cruz, a city in which I had never been. I only knew it was surrounded by redwood forests and on the shores of Monterey Bay. All of this somehow penetrated my conscious or unconscious mind to the extent that I came home one day and said to my daughter, Dianne, who had been living with me for several years, for her husband had died a few months prior to George's death, "How would you like to move to Santa Cruz?" She said, "Not now, Mother, but I have always planned to retire in the Northern California area." This was a surprise to me, but also a joy for I knew that someday we would both be living in that area. The next morning I made a date with a realtor to look at homes in Santa Cruz. The fact that I had never been there did not bother me at all. Actually if anyone had told me a month before that I would leave my friends, my activities in which I was involved, my lovely home and Los Angeles, a city I love, I would have said they were crazy. At that time, however, I didn't think or analyze, I just moved.

The following weekend Dianne, Ann Chamberlain, and I set off to drive to Santa Cruz, about a six-hour drive from Los Angeles. We met a realtor named Arnoldo Gil-Osorio, who had been recommended to us as having sold more houses than anyone else in the nation for several years running. I thought this was an exaggeration, but later learned that it was true. We met him in his office at 3:00 p.m. He sat down at his computer while we waited rather impatiently. He told us later that he had to check out all of the listings because houses were selling so fast that he did not want to show us anything which had already been sold. This was surely the top of the real estate market—until now, that is. We saw several rather mediocre houses from my point of view, for the amount I wanted to pay. Obviously Mr. Gil-Osorio knew I was not impressed. He then said to me, "Now that I have met you, I know exactly what you would like, but it is more than you indicated you wanted to pay." I said, "Let's look." We drove up the driveway to one house, and found a beautiful long bridge over a magnificent waterfall with lovely ferns and flowers. As we walked over the bridge to steps leading to the house, I said, "This is my house, I will buy it." At that Mr. Gil-Osorio said, "It is a beautiful house, but there are too many steps for you at your age." This never occurred to me and I responded by saying, "They will keep me young." As we opened the front door, I was even more enthralled and I found it to be simple, serene and beautiful, and very modern, reminding me of a Frank Lloyd Wright house. It was high enough on the lot to have a magnificent view of the Monterey Bay. What I didn't learn until after I had purchased the house was an extra dividend, a building in the rear with an enclosed lap pool. My children and I love to swim. In fact, when they were young they were being trained as Olympic swimmers. The pool was very expensive to heat plus my daughters made me promise I would never swim unless someone else was with me. This made it very easy for me to turn this building into a charming apartment for Dianne, with the hope that she would indeed move to Santa Cruz. This she did in 1993, and she now works happily in the Chancellor's Office at UCSC.

Now I must go back and tell you about my financial situation at the time I purchased my house. My house in Santa Monica was paid for, but after paying the Motion Picture Home, and other expenses after George's death, I had exactly $20,000 in the bank. This was in addition to my monthly payments from Social Security and the university pension, which is only enough to live on rather modestly. The fact was that I was buying a $650,000 house did not bother me a bit, for I knew I would sell my Santa Monica house. When, or for how much, I did not question. I was surprised when Mr. Gil-Osorio would not close the deal until the following morning. He was convinced that I was a little crazy to make up my mind so fast, and indeed I was, from a realistic point of view. Nevertheless, I gave him $10,000 and asked him to draw up the necessary papers and the balance would be forthcoming.

We returned home in a state of euphoria. I never once had a feeling of anxiety for I knew I was making the right move, although I didn't ask why. I was moving without any thought of what I was really doing. I was changing my whole life, giving up an environment I knew, moving to a city in which I had never been before. The only people I knew in Santa Cruz were John Robbins and his family whom I had just met, my friend who was volunteering for John, and Mr. Gil-Osorio, my real-estate agent who is now my neighbor and very good friend.

Of course, my friends were appalled, especially after eighty of them had just given me an eightieth birthday party only a year before. What an event that was! It was given at a beautiful hotel in Santa Monica, a combination of cocktails and supper. My very dear friend, Celeste Holm, the illustrious actress, flew once more from New York to be Mistress of Ceremonies. Films were presented of my life and amazing tributes were given by special friends, including Norman Cousins, who had been editor of the Saturday Review for many years and was then a member of the faculty at UCLA. There were three-hundred friends attending. Others were attending a dinner at another hotel for the Prince of Wales. Not many of us have been in competition with a prince! Mine was a magnificently planned and executed party by my friends, Marjorie Fasman,

Lois Howard, Lisa Citron, Claire Townsend, and others. I cannot fail to speak of the table centerpieces. There were fifteen-inch high cutout figures of me at 80, with another figure of me at ten peeking over the shoulder of the first cutout figure. These were surrounded by beautiful flowers. I believe this idea came from the creative and ingenious mind of Marjorie Fasman. I do not know, however, who dreamed up the idea for my birthday gift, but what a gift it was! A $25,000 check to give away! Of course I was stunned by such generosity and the ability to make gifts to those organizations working for peace and against the continuation of the arms race. The money had actually been placed in a foundation, so I made choices and checks were then sent in my name. I also have a huge book with letters from friends across the world, which my children will inherit.

And now I was leaving all my friends to move four-hundred miles away! The day I put my house on the market was the day I sold it to the first person who looked at it for the price I was asking: $850,000. Several people were at the door wanting to see the house, but I had already verbally agreed to sell it to the first bidder. A lady came up to me and said, "I will pay you $15,000 more than anyone else." I said I had already agreed to take the first offer from a man who loved the house and the garden, and I liked him. The man who had just made this offer said, "Thank goodness there are still people who care more about people than money."

I tell you this because shortly after the deal was closed, the man who bought the house learned that the extra room he had planned to build for his office was more than he could afford, so he turned around and sold the house to the lady who would give me more money, for $902.000. As it happened, the house was in escrow for three months and the lady could not come up with the money. Think what would have happened to me if I had cared more about money than people! This taught me again that we must always follow the dictates of our hearts. Even today, I do not know how I was able to do this so totally, but I did, and have never regretted it for one moment. This does not mean that I did not have a tinge of anxiety, but only for one day. When I told my dear neighbor across the street, whose four children I had seen grow up, that I was moving away, she began to cry. All of a sudden I asked myself why I was leaving my beautiful home, my friends and the work I was doing. For the rest of that day I was so full of anxiety such as I had never in my life felt before that I had dysentery. When I went to bed that night I said, "Oh, please help me, I cannot live this way!" The next morning I awakened feeling happy and refreshed. The message I had received from my own consciousness or from a higher source was, "Never look backward, always look forward. You can stay in your little house here and lead a good life, but down the road you will live to regret it." From that day on, I have moved with joy in my heart which has never left me.

Chapter Seventeen

Someday, after we have mastered the winds, the waves, the tides, and gravity, we shall harness for God the energies of love. Then, for the second time in history of the world, man will have discovered fire.

—*Pierre Teilhard de Chardin*

I moved into my house in Santa Cruz on June 14, 1989, just four months before the big earthquake. My darling Dianne left her work at Petersen Publishing Company, where she was a graphic designer, long enough to help me move. Getting settled was gratifying, for all my furniture and art objects looked as if they had been designed for my new home.

After about a week, Dianne returned to Los Angeles and now I was alone. As I look back, it was the first time in my life I had ever lived alone. Somehow I did not seem to feel lonely for I was where I needed to be. Anyway, how could one be lonely surrounded by so much beauty!

Somehow I don't really remember those first days. All I remember are the highlights. I soon learned that I had a very close friend of many years ago living in Santa Cruz. Her name was Ruth Engel. She and her husband, Sam, a writer and producer at 20th Century-Fox, had been close friends before and during the Second World War. They had moved north, but I never really knew exactly where—Santa Cruz, Santa Clara—somewhere up north. During my move, as I was throwing away cards which came to me after George's death, I found one from Ruth Engel with a return address from Santa Cruz. I was overwhelmed with joy. I had a close friend in Santa Cruz! We even lived very close to one another. She was alone, too, for Sam had died the same year as my George did.

The next big memory was a luncheon given by Diane Klein, a friend of one of my dearest friends in L.A., Suzy Marks. Diane invited only seven people to have luncheon in the gazebo 'midst the large expanse of lawn surrounded by gardens with an exquisite view of the Monterey Bay. Diane was so wise, for she invited individuals who were active in doing important things for our world and our earth. We were small enough in number to get to know one another as well as our mutual interests. One of those individuals, a lady with a lovely Irish accent named Sheila Stuart, soon had another luncheon for me. What a day that was! There were approximately twenty guests, the Mayor of Santa Cruz, the Chief Librarian at UCSC, leaders in various fields, all active in making this city the remarkable one it is. During luncheon Sheila asked each of us to tell where we were born and a brief history of our lives. Not only did I become aware and acquainted with my new friends, but they learned more about one another than they had known before. I have since used this technique to acquaint people with one another, which opens many doors.

The summer passed in making new friends and entertaining friends visiting me from Los Angeles. Someone asked me if I didn't miss all my friends there. I responded in the negative for I said, "No, because I am now having quality time when they visit me and not sitting around a table at meetings." Of course, there are many I do miss for not all of them have visited me. I go back for visits rather frequently and manage to see as many as possible. I think friends are too precious to lose, so I always try to keep in contact through letters, telephone, or visits.

My first visit back was on October 15, 1989, when I was honored by the Southern California Chapter of Physicians for Social Responsibility at a beautiful garden party in Brentwood. I was given a most impressive crystal award which reads: "The Los Angeles Physicians for Social Responsibility Honors Eleanor Wasson, Healer of the Planet. We are proud to have this exceptional woman for her singular dedication to the protection of the planet and her vision of a world without war."

Two nights later on October 17, the Loma Prieta earthquake struck the whole northern California area. We stood in front of the TV set and saw the total devastation of Santa Cruz. I thought, of course, that my modern glass house would be no more. My daughter, Joan, was in L.A. for the honor I had just received, so she canceled her appointments and the two of us drove back to Santa Cruz. We saw many chimneys down along the way and other devastation, but when we walked into my house we saw only a few books off the shelves. After looking further, we saw the large and very heavy rosewood chest in my living room about five inches from the wall, but the porcelain plate and other fragile articles were intact. In my bathroom I had a huge conch shell on the back of my toilet which was about six feet into the room, but not a single bottle fell over. It was like a message telling me that a power was there, but did not hurt me. I had another such miracle in 1995 about which I shall tell you.

Life in Santa Cruz continued to be an adventure, with new friends all along the way. Shortly after my arrival I was invited to become a board member for the Santa Cruz Environmental Council. My only contribution was to help raise funds by inviting Helen Caldicott to come to Santa Cruz as a speaker at the Santa Cruz Auditorium. Our mutual friend, Jerry Jampolsky, psychiatrist and author of "Love is Letting Go of Fear," brought Helen from San Francisco to my house. I shall never forget his entrance as he stood on the landing of the steps leading to my living room when he said, "Eleanor, your house is full of angels!" I had always said this was so, but if a psychiatrist says this, it must be so. Later I shall tell you that indeed my house is full of angels.

Chapter Seventeen

One day a new friend, Gail Ow, called and asked if I would be interested in becoming a member of the Board of Trustees for the University of California Santa Cruz Foundation. What an honor this was! I was surprised that such an invitation would come to me. Of course I said "Yes." When I attended my first meeting, I found the President was Anne Levin, a most wonderful and creative lady who remains one of my most special and beloved friends. I remained on the board for five years, after which time I resigned for I felt I had little to offer other than my deep interest in the university. I continue to attend events and have found a wonderful friend in the former Chancellor, M.R.C. Greenwood, now Provost and Vice President of the University of California system, truly a great lady.

It was quite natural after meeting John Robbins and introducing him at the symposium in Los Angeles prior to my moving here, that he and his lovely wife, Deo, would become friends. I visited them at their house and learned an organization called EarthSave was in the process of being formed. It would be designed from John's book, "Diet for a New America," in order to educate people about the affects of our food choices upon the environment. It was to begin its operations in the garage of Sue Cliff, a lovely young woman who was always in the front of good causes not only at home, but throughout the world. I volunteered to help with calls, files, and letter writing. Soon thereafter, Patricia Carney established the offices and became the

Executive Director. She brought her prior experience of running a small nonprofit and thirteen years as a stage and company manager for off and on Broadway productions, including "A Chorus Line." Both Pat and John realized they needed a board of directors, so I was among those asked to participate. On the board were two people who also moved from Los Angeles, Ian and Terry Thiermann. Ian had established a production company for documentary films. He was an associate producer for "Women Speak for America and for the World," which won an Oscar at the Academy of Motion Picture Arts and Sciences.

Ian and I were most interested in raising money for the Foundation, so we offered to produce several events at the Santa Cruz Civic Auditorium. The first event presented Deepak Chopra, who had promised John that he would speak in behalf of the Foundation without charging a fee. This allowed us to bring quite a sum of money to EarthSave. The next one was Robert Kennedy, Jr., who had done so much in restoring the Hudson River from a highly polluted one to the clearest body of water in North America—all done by the cooperation of the total community against the polluters. Our last lecture was given by Marianne Williamson, leading to a friendship which opened new doors in my life, about which I shall tell you later.

Chapter Eighteen

*We have grasped the mystery of the atom and
rejected the Sermon on the Mount. Ours is a
world of nuclear giants and ethical infants. We
know more about war than we know about peace,
more about Killing than we know about living.*

—*General Omar Bradley*

The night of December 13, 1995 is a memorable
one. It began with a small birthday celebration for our
friend, Lynne Rice. While it was warm and cozy inside,
there was a terrific rain and windstorm outside. It was
so drastic, in fact, that we asked those who lived a dis-
tance away to spend the night. One of them was Lynne.
I asked Lynne if she would like to sleep in the roll-down
bed in the library or in the twin next to me. She chose
the latter even though I was surprised that she wouldn't
prefer the privacy of the library. She told me later that
she herself didn't know why she made that decision.

By 1:00 a.m. everyone was sound asleep under
warm quilts. All of this changed when at 4:15 a.m.
there was a tremendous sound and shaking of the
house. My friend, Lynne, jumped out of bed. I quickly
assured her, however, that all was well. I said, "Lynne,
that was the worst earthquake I have ever felt, but it's

over already." Nevertheless, we went out into the hall to find our other friends appalled by what they were seeing—as we were, too. The ceiling and the lights were out in the hall and as we moved further into the living area, we saw the trunk and branches of an enormous tree which had fallen into the house over the library where Lynne would have been sleeping. All the walls and ceilings were down throughout the library, hall and living room. Rain was still pouring.

As we huddled together in the cold, our immediate reaction was one of gratitude that no one was hurt even though we were in a state of shock. We called 911 and firemen arrived 'midst the heavy sounds of sirens, arousing surrounding neighbors—one of whom was Arnoldo Gil-Osorio, who took us all to his large house down the hill.

As I went to my house the next morning, I found a young carpenter, a very humble and gentle man who had helped me with odd jobs about the house and garden. He said, "Eleanor, I will do anything in the world to help you." I knew he was without a job and no doubt needed one, so he was made head of the demolition crew. I have always said the falling of that tree brought about a number of miracles, the first one being that we were not hurt, the second was full work for my friend who needed it very badly.

Fortunately, good insurance covered all the house and property losses. One of their representatives came the following day to my neighbor's house where I stayed for many months until the house was rebuilt. This representative could not have been more helpful. She immediately wrote out a check to cover my living expenses amounting to twice as much as my university pension and my social security. The company undoubtedly realized I could not rent a place comparable to my own home, so allowed for this.

A few days later at breakfast in my friend's house, my hostess said they had some unfortunate business problems and they were several months behind in their mortgage payments and were about to lose their home. The rent which I was able to pay them as a result of the insurance payment enabled them to save their home, which is still theirs. This was like a miracle, as were the above.

I continued going to the house for the first few days as work progressed. The first things workers had to do was remove, pack and itemize everything in the house to store during the rebuilding, as well as move out all of the damaged and the destroyed furniture, rugs, lamps, etc.

When the tree fell, my house was badly in need of painting, which I could never have afforded with my limited income, but by the time I moved back on August 1, 1996, I had a new house in every aspect, thanks to my insurance. Also, thanks to my decorator, Emily Novak from San Francisco, I had beautiful new furnishings. Of course, I was distressed because none of my precious art objects were on the itemized list among those things to be stored. I assumed they had all been destroyed. With the unpacking, however, they all turned up. One was the bronze Tibetan Buddha, a gift of peace and serenity, which was sitting on one end of my fireplace. It was totally undamaged, while at the other end of the fireplace had been a bronze vase that was replaceable. It was flattened as if a train had run over it. Was this a miracle? All my beautiful silver and crystal awards were intact, even though they were sitting under a lamp which had been demolished. They all appeared again even though they were not itemized as having been found. Were the angels there?

Now my house has been totally rebuilt, and refurnished more beautifully than before. It is a true Shangri-la. It will continue being a meeting place for all who care about one another and the magnificent world in which we live. Are there miracles? Are there angels? It is for you to guess. I believe there are.

Chapter Nineteen

If you give not help to others, you are
wasting those prayers to Buddha.

—Chinese Proverb

In the first chapter of my story, I referred to the great changes taking place causing a new awakening in the lives of people around the world. The vast spaces between the rich and the poor across our planet are not only causing more poverty, starvation, disease and death, but also unrest, increased violence and striking out against injustice. It is the failure of our leaders to listen to the voices and the needs of the people. Each of you reading these lines knows about what I speak. You know, too, the state of our environment and the plundering of our natural resources. We are also seeing more and more natural disasters around the globe, such as hurricanes, earthquakes and floods. I believe we have reached a point in history when the choices we make can destroy us or take us into a world in which we have learned that all life is as sacred as our own. Either way, however, I fear will be full of pain.

Will it take more natural disasters, a world in turmoil and possibly a financial depression to awaken those in power to begin to take responsibility toward the whole of life?

Fortunately, I believe voices are being heard. The protests from individuals, members of unions and NGOs against inadequacies of the current global governance were heard throughout the world at the World Trade Organization Conference in Seattle in late 1999, in Washington, D.C. in early 2000, and again in Cancun, Mexico in 2003. The State of the World Forum and other groups are gathering thousands of individuals together to address common concerns and common problems. The programs presented by The Natural Step, based in San Francisco, are going far in educating leaders in top industries relative to their part in polluting the lands, skies and seas. Paul Hawken, Amory and Hunter Lovins have told us in their book, "Natural Capitalism," of the many developments in production which will change the destruction of our environment which is now taking place. In addition, I believe we are all seeing and feeling a rising sense of consciousness on the part of individuals toward one another and the Earth.

My own interests in the environment have and are taking me to conferences and meetings across the land helping me to take action wherever I can. One of the greatest conferences I have ever attended was in Washington, D.C., at Georgetown University, presented by Marianne Williamson, Neale Walsch and the Center for Visionary Leadership. I mentioned earlier about sharing philosophies with Marianne when she was in Santa Cruz several years ago. As a result, she invited me to become a member of a committee being formed by the Center for Visionary Leadership in Washington, D.C. Members of the Committee met in various locations for four years, culminating in the Conference at Georgetown University in April of 2000. Why was this was one of the greatest conferences I have ever attended? It was the first time I have ever seen several hundred individuals totally committed to the fact that we are all one and have the ability to bring about change through knowledge, love and compassion. Many national leaders were there and spoke most eloquently, with standing ovations for each one as their words touched the hearts and minds of all of us. Robert Kennedy, Jr., John Vasconcellos (California State Senator for thirty-five years), Neale Walsch, Marianne Williamson, Claudine Schneider (former Congresswoman), John Hagelin, Ph.D. (candidate for U.S. President), and many other national leaders who are totally dedicated to restoring the dreams of our founding fathers. Listening and learning are not enough, however, but do inspire us to action. Such conferences do indeed do that. Speaking out, writing, and acting in behalf of justice must become as important as breathing, for indeed our actions affect the whole of life.

Another great conference I attended was the State of the World Forum, which took place in New York City in September 2000. Leaders from across the world were in attendance, including many young people, our leaders for tomorrow.

The State of the World Forum, whose president is Jim Garrison, was inspired by Mikhail Gorbachev, who opened the sessions with many wise statements. He said, in essence, that globalization is a process and we need to have it, but we need to find new ways so it can become an advantage to all people. Today, unfortunately, large corporations are benefiting the most, causing an ever-widening gap between the rich and the poor. He said that the United Nations must be protected—and not just for the powerful, but for the benefit of all people. Presentations during the eight days of this forum stressed the banning of all nuclear weapons, education for children across the world, eliminating starvation and hunger, and working to save the environment. Over and over again, the 2,000 individuals attending this forum heard national and international leaders speak about these issues and the many new programs being developed around the world that are working to bring about change in human consciousness and envisioning a better world for all life on this planet.

Chapter Twenty

Anyone who does not believe in
miracles is not a realist.

—David Ben-Gurion

The longer we live the more aware we become relative to the miracles in our lives. Always is the miracle of life all around us, the trees, the flowers, the magnitude and beauties of nature. How often we have watched a flock of birds flying in unison, rising in the sky as one, and schools of fish gliding together in harmony with one another.

Recently, I have been looking back upon what we might call minor miracles, but nevertheless tell us again that we are all one and everything is energy.

Some years ago my friends, Cathy Dees and Kay Croissant, spent a winter in Verona, Italy, home of Romeo and Juliet. They stayed in a 15th Century villa which had been modernized without in any way destroying its original beauty. I had the privilege of visiting them while they were there. One day we took the train to Venice, which is not far from Verona. We spent a wonderful day exploring the history and beauties of this enchanting city. We had lunch in a beautiful restaurant on the plaza, which we were told Lord Byron and his friends frequented, enjoying food, wine, and conversation. A few days after our visit I had an urge to return to Venice alone. I wanted to explore further and feast on the antiquities of this magical place. This I did, losing all sense of time. Shortly after 2:00 o'clock I realized I was hungry, so I went into the nearest restaurant. After being seated and given a menu, I said to myself, "Why am I here, I must go across the plaza to Lord Byron's restaurant." This I did, and was seated at one of the tables on one side of a long narrow room with tables on each side. Being past the luncheon hour, there were few people dining. Right across from me were a young man and woman speaking English. I couldn't help commenting and said, "How good to hear English spoken after three weeks of hearing mostly Italian." We spoke together for a few moments. I learned that she was from England and was in Italy studying opera. Finally we stood up and she and I embraced and at the same moment we both said, "How wonderful to see you again!" We exchanged names and addresses and a few months later she came to the U.S. to visit me. Was this an old friend from another lifetime? I believe so, but how do you explain it?

Another minor miracle happened when I was still living in Santa Monica after George's death. It happened on my birthday. When my mother was living, I always sent pink roses in appreciation for her love and caring. When I awakened that day, I said to myself, "I wish my mother were here so I could send pink roses." About one hour later the doorbell rang and a delivery man gave me a dozen pink roses. My new friend, Joseph Lebenzon, who was working with me and others against the arms race, knew it was my birthday, but he knew nothing about the pink roses. How did he get the message? I hardly knew him at that time.

Another flower story happened recently, as I was preparing for dinner guests. Everything was ready, but I had to go out to get flowers for the living room and dining room table. I put water in the vases and was about to leave the house when the doorbell rang and a young friend stood at the door and handed me two bouquets. Do we have a connection with all other life and do we "tune in" to another's needs if we are receptive? I think so. In fact, we all have them, but often we take such happenings for granted.

Another time, I was out of computer paper, so I went to the village to buy it. At the same time, I was having guests for dinner and had a number of other errands to run. When I arrived home I realized I had forgotten the paper. I was much annoyed with myself, but it was too late to go back. When my guests arrived, one of them handed me a package of computer paper, the same brand as I always buy. I said with amazement, "Phyllis, you usually bring flowers, what made you buy this paper?' She gently said, "I just knew you needed it." Explain this one. Are we not all one in a pool of consciousness?

Some years ago I was planning my third trip to Egypt. I was going with friends from Los Angeles but planned to meet my dear young friend, Ann McFarlene, from Australia. The day before we left L.A. I had a call from Ann saying she could not meet me as planned and would not be making the trip. After my other friends and I had been in Cairo a few days, I was in one of the shops. When I looked up, there was Ann in the midst of a population of 17 million people. Her plans had changed again but she had no way of reaching me, as we had already left. Once again, could it be that we were on the same energy and our love brought us together? Yes, I am a believer in miracles and it is always wonderful turning the impossible into the possible.

Chapter Twenty-One

If ever the world sees a time when women
shall come together purely and simply for
the benefit of mankind, it will be a power
such as the world has never known.

—*Matthew Arnold*

As I come toward the end of this book I feel I must share an experience I have had during the past two years. It started as a result of a plea by my dear friend, Marianne Williamson, the remarkable author, who has pleaded with individuals everywhere to really get to know one another through conversations in groups. She suggested getting six or eight friends to sit down and talk, to really learn about one another. While I wasn't quite sure what this would mean, I love and respect Marianne so much I decided to try it.

About two years ago, I invited seven friends for an afternoon meeting at my house for conversations and really learning to know one another even though we thought we already did. It took us two 2-hour sessions, however, to really "get acquainted." We learned where we were born, went to school and most of all what we had done with our lives and what we had achieved. We realized that we really hadn't known one another at all and what we really learned was that we had power. We were achievers and had successes all along the way. Few women, as I said before, realize all the skills we learn by being a mother and running a household successfully.

Frankly, we were amazed to realize how many of our achievements we had taken for granted. We then decided to meet for two hours one late afternoon a week. We began by "checking in," speaking for one or two minutes on any subject we pleased with no interruptions and with the understanding that our words were sacred and would not be repeated. As time progressed we learned more and more how much power we had and must direct it toward healing the planet and working for peace in every way we could. We named our group WomenRise for Global Peace.

Our first public venture was on November 11, 2002, a Celebration for Peace event by the San Lorenzo River in one of our public parks. We knew that every action we took must be positive and therefore be for peace. It was a real celebration with music, dancing and togetherness helping us to realize that we are all one in a world where peace must be attained if we are to survive.

More and more individuals have wanted to join our group, which has made it necessary for us to train others to form their own groups, to learn from one another, to share and to grow.

This has been a remarkable experience. There are

now twenty of us from the original group. We range in age from thirty to ninety-six, all having or having had interesting careers. The love and respect we have for one another is profound. We are all different, but when we come together it is as if we were one. No action is ever taken without complete agreement, reached with relative ease due to our increasing ability to really listen to one another. This process has been compared to the ancient Indian Grandmother's Council. We are open to assist in any situation or individual needing help and understanding.

Never in my 96 years have I worked with a group where total love exists with understanding and laughter all along the way. One of our group has been away and wrote the following: "I have been thinking a lot about WomenRise and the way anything which is brought to the group is met with respect, enthusiasm and complete support...immediately. Secondly, the energy and commitment which is put into events and causes evokes a deep admiration within me. With such busy and full lives, to find the time and to commit so deeply and fully to the events scheduled is something beautiful and meaningful to experience."

We have no officers or by-laws, but tremendous harmony and sharing. I urge you, the reader, to gather a few of your friends for conversation and really get to know one another. It is like magic if you can truly share what is in your heart.

Chapter Twenty-Two

*The topic of unselfish love has been
placed on the agenda of history and is
about to become its main business.*

—*Pitirim Sorokin*

As I look back upon my life, I am extremely grateful
and sometimes wonder at my good fortune all along the
way. I am sure that my entrance into this world and my
early years have much to do with it. Having intelligent
and loving parents played a key role. I am more aware
of this each day as I find so few friends and acquaintances who have had happy childhoods some happy
perhaps, but without a real tie of affection and feelings
of gratitude for their parents.

This book is ending at a time when we are seeing
tremendous differences in the hearts and minds of people here and across the world. We are seeing the effects
of angers, frustrations, fears and poverty resulting in
terrorism such as 9/11. To me it was a strike against
capitalism: the World Trade Center, the military, the
Pentagon and, if one flight had not been aborted, our
government, the White House.

As a result we are now at war. Our leaders in Washington chose to strike back instead of having the heart and the vision to see long range, to negotiate with our neighbors across the lands and seas. No one knows what the future will bring. Our challenges are great as we endeavor to seek new leaders who will replace fear and hate with love and compassion. There is absolutely no way negative actions can bring positive results.

Recently, I read a statement by Bertrand Russell, who said, "I have lived in pursuit of a vision, both personal and social: personal, to care for what is noble, for what is beautiful, for what is gentle, to allow moments of insight to give wisdom at more mundane times; social, to see in imagination the society that is to be created, where individuals grow freely, and where hate and greed and envy die because there is nothing to nourish them. These things I believe, and the world, for all its horrors, has left me unshaken."

I was very taken by this statement and while I could never have expressed it so eloquently, I have had somewhat the same philosophy, inherited from my parents through their love.

Now as I look back upon the events of the past century, I am full of ecstasy for all that has been accomplished technologically to enhance the lives of each of us, gifts which could benefit every living soul, but have not. Now I ask myself each day what would be the most important thing I could do in my remaining years to help raise the consciousness both for myself and others across the world. I do believe each of us has the power to make change by our positive thoughts and actions. Sometimes I am inclined to talk about negative happenings. I fear that as we do this we are giving energy to that negative action. I tell myself I must be aware of the negative but rather focus on the positive and what we can do to bring about the changes that are needed.

As I see more and more pollution of the environment, an ever widening financial gap between the rich and the poor, the continuing battles across the world, violence and poverty in our own nation, I find it difficult to always dwell on the positive. I can only do this because I believe so completely in the evolution of the individual mind and soul. We are given opportunities all along the way to make our own choices. We learn by living and living again and again. Our lessons, as I have said, are many—tolerance, humility, understanding, obedience, faith, charity, compassion, and the greatest of all is love. The Universal power, or God if you choose, gives us free will and free choice in all we do, but always with the law of cause and effect. We reap what we sow. I have a feeling that we are about to learn many lessons by the actions we have made all along the way, bringing us where we are today. I do not think the next years are going to be easy ones, but they will be serious learning ones. I believe, however, that we will emerge with a greater knowledge of the fact that we are all one and must share and work with one another if we are to survive.

I think we are seeing the results of much we have done and are doing to the Earth—floods, hurricanes, weather changes, landslides, high tides, polluted air and water. These should be, and I believe are, wake-up calls. I have faith that there are enough people who are aware and taking action to bring about change. There is a higher consciousness arising across the world. Another wonderful thing is happening of which we should all be aware—watch the babies being born today. They are aware and intelligent beyond any we have ever seen before. It is my belief that these are the souls who will be here as leaders to welcome the changes in thinking and action, to open the doors to a civilization where love prevails and each person's needs are respected as their own. I do not believe change will happen overnight or without pain, but we will learn.

For myself, I look forward to as many years as I am productive and in my own way can be an influence for good. Each of us has that power. Recognize each person we meet as a friend, listen to them and take action in their behalf. Write letters or call our representatives, the President, corporation presidents and all those who are making decisions which affect us all. Take time to cherish the beauties of this world and be thankful. These are but a few of the actions we can take each day of our lives. With it all, we must have a vision of the world in which we want to live and, like Bertrand Russell, be unshaken by the horrors we see today and know that we have the power to make change.

I should like to share an example of the power of one letter. I am sure you remember New Year's Eve day and evening in the year 2000 when we watched television with people around the world, singing, dancing and laughing with no political or religious agenda. I was so overwhelmed by the joy demonstrated by millions of citizens in all countries that I shared my joy with my friend Jane Olson, president of the Human Rights Watch and Landmine Survivors, who said, "Why don't you write to my friend, Tom Johnson, who is CEO for the television station CNN?" This I did, thanking him for the wonderful coverage on his station. I not only had a personally written thank-you card from him, but I learned later that he had my letter copied and sent it to every employee of CNN across the world. We really seldom know the power of one small letter.

As I close this story of my life and my philosophy, I am grateful to you, the reader. No one expects to live as long as I have, at least I didn't. I find it rather amazing. While I am not as agile as I would like to be, I have good hearing and vision, for which I am most grateful. I enjoy every moment of my life, my two wonderful daughters, eight grandchildren, nine great-grandchildren, and my friends across the globe. I maintain those friendships through visits and correspondence. The philosopher, Kahlil Gibran, said, "One who ceases to be a friend has never been one." I therefore believe we must keep contact with our friends, cherishing the fact that they are there.

One event which will remain the greatest honor of my life took place on May 31, 2000. My friends, Pauline and Richard Saxon, who some years ago received the Albert Schweitzer Award for their great work with Physicians for Social Responsibility, were primarily responsible. I was given the Lifetime Achievement Award by this organization at a dinner at the Beverly Hilton Hotel in Beverly Hills along with the scientist and cofounder of Sun Microsystems, Bill Joy; the writer, activist, and teacher Norman Corwin; and Chairman, Board of Trustees, W. Alton Jones Foundation, Dr. Bradford W. Edgerton. Many words were written and spoken on that memorable evening. I want to share only a few of them, which I shall carry in my heart as long as I live with the promise that I continue to restrain my ego. "Dearest Eleanor, you are a spiritual magnet whose force changes people and alters their way of thinking to exercise their better selves. It is a miracle that at ninety-two you are still vital and strong sending your message of faith in human potential."

I continue to say that we all have power providing every action is motivated by love. And yes, a sense of humor.